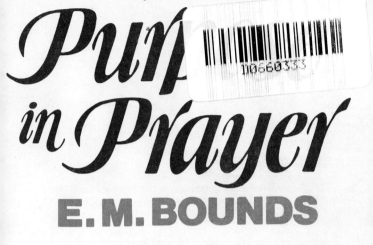

Pur... in Prayer

E. M. BOUNDS

MOODY PRESS

CHICAGO

All scripture quotations in this book are from the
American Standard Version (1901).

ISBN: 0-8024-6949-3

Printed in the United States of America

CONTENTS

INTRODUCTION

EDWARD McKENDREE BOUNDS was born in Shelby County, Missouri, August 15, 1835, and died August 24, 1913, in Washington, Georgia. He received his public school education at Shelbyville and was admitted to the bar after his twenty-first birthday. He practiced law until called to preach the Gospel at the age of tweny-four. His first pastorate was the Monticello, Missouri, circuit. It was while he served as pastor of Brunswick, Missouri, that war was declared, and the young minister was made a prisoner of war because he would not take the oath of allegiance to the federal government. He was sent to St. Louis and later transferred to Memphis, Tennessee.

Finally securing his release, he traveled on foot nearly one hundred miles to join General Pierce's command in Mississippi and was soon after made chaplain of the Fifth Missouri Regiment, a position he held until near the close of the war, when he was captured and held as prisoner at Nashville, Tennessee.

After the war, the Reverend E. M. Bounds was pastor of churches in Tennessee and Alabama. In 1875 he was assigned to St. Paul Methodist Church in St. Louis and served there for four years. In 1876 he was married to Emmie Barnette at Eufaula, Alabama, who died ten years later. In 1887 he was married to Hattie Barnette, who, with five children, survived him.

After serving several pastorates, he was sent to the First Methodist Church in St. Louis for one year and to St.

Paul Methodist Church for three years. At the end of his
pastorate, he became the editor of the St. Louis *Christian
Advocate.*

He was a forceful writer and a very deep thinker. He
spent the last seventeen years of his life with his family
in Washington, Georgia. Most of the time he was reading,
writing and praying. He rose at four A.M. each day for
many years and was indefatigable in his study of the Bible.
His writings were read by thousands of people and were
in demand by the church people of every Protestant denomination.

Bounds was the embodiment of humility, with a se-
raphic devotion to Jesus Christ. He reached that high
place where self is forgotten and the love of God and humanity was the all-absorbing thought and purpose. At
seventy-six years of age he came to me in Brooklyn, New
York, and so intense was he that he awoke us at three
o'clock in the morning, praying and weeping over the
lost of the earth. All during the day he would go into the
church next door and be found on his knees until called
for his meals. This is what he called the "business of praying." Infused with this heavenly ozone, he wrote *Preacher
and Prayer,* a classic in its line, and now in several foreign
languages, read by men and women all over the world.
In 1909, while the Reverend A. C. Dixon was preaching
in Dr. Broughton's Tabernacle, Atlanta, Georgia, I sent
him a copy of *Preacher and Prayer,* by Bounds. He said:

"This little book was given me by a friend. I received
another copy at Christmas from another friend. 'Well,'
thought I, 'there must be something worth while in the
little book, or two of my friends would not have selected
the same present for me.' So I read the first page until I
came to the words: 'Man is looking for better methods,

God is looking for better men. Man is God's method.'
That was enough for me and my appetite demanded more
until the book was finished with pleasure."

This present volume is a companion work, and reflects
the true spirit of a man whose business it was to live the
Gospel that he preached. He was not a luminary but a
sun and takes his place with Brainerd and Bramwell as
untiring intercessors with God.

H. W. HODGE

* * *

*My Creed leads me to think that prayer is efficacious,
and surely a day's asking God to overrule all events for
good is not lost. Still there is a great feeling that when
a man is praying he is doing nothing, and this feeling
makes us give undue importance to work, sometimes even
to the hurrying over or even to the neglect of prayer.*

*Do not we rest in our day too much on the arm of flesh?
Cannot the same wonders be done now as of old? Do not
the eyes of the Lord run to and fro throughout the whole
earth still to show Himself strong on behalf of those who
put their trust in Him? Oh that God would give me more
practical faith in Him! Where is now the Lord God of
Elijah? He is waiting for Elijah to call on Him.*

JAMES GILMOUR OF MONGOLIA

1

GOD SHAPES THE WORLD
BY PRAYER

THE MORE PRAYING there is in the world, the better the world will be, the mightier the forces against evil everywhere. Prayer, in one phase of its operation, is a disinfectant and a preventive. It purifies the air; it destroys the contagion of evil. Prayer is no fitful, short-lived thing. It is no voice crying unheard and unheeded in the silence. It is a voice which goes into God's ear, and it lives as long as God's ear is open to holy pleas, as long as God's heart is alive to holy things.

God shapes the world by prayer. Prayers are deathless. The lips that uttered them may be closed in death, the heart that felt them may have ceased to beat, but the prayers live before God, and God's heart is set on them and prayers outlive the lives of those who uttered them; they outlive a generation, outlive an age, outlive a world.

That man is the most immortal who has done the most and the best praying. They are God's heroes, God's saints, God's servants, God's vicegerents. A man can pray better because of the prayers of the past; a man can live holier because of the prayers of the past; the man of many and acceptable prayers has done the truest and greatest service to the incoming generation. The prayers of God's saints strengthen the unborn generation against the desolating waves of sin and evil. Woe to the generation of sons who

9

find their censers empty of the rich incense of prayer, whose fathers have been too busy or too unbelieving to pray, and perils inexpressible and consequences untold are their unhappy heritage. Fortunate are they whose fathers and mothers have left them a wealthy patrimony of prayer.

The prayers of God's saints are the capital stock in heaven by which Christ carries on His great work upon earth. The great throes and mighty convulsions on earth are the results of these prayers. Earth is changed, revolutionized, angels move on more powerful and rapid wing, and God's policy is shaped as the prayers are more numerous, more efficient.

It is true that the mightiest successes that come to God's cause are created and carried on by prayer. God's day of power; the angelic days of activity and power are when God's Church comes into its mightiest inheritance of mightiest faith and mightiest prayer. God's conquering days are when the saints have given themselves to mightiest prayer. When God's house on earth is a house of prayer, then God's house in heaven is busy and all-potent in its plans and movements; then His earthly armies are clothed with the triumphs and spoils of victory and His enemies defeated on every hand.

God conditions the very life and prosperity of His cause on prayer. The condition was put in the very existence of God's cause in this world. *Ask of me* is the one condition God puts in the very advance and triumph of His cause.

Men are to pray—to pray for the advance of God's cause. Prayer puts God in full force in the world. To a prayerful man, God is present in realized force; to a prayerful church, God is present in glorious power, and

Psalm 2 is the divine description of the establishment of God's cause through Jesus Christ. All inferior dispensations have merged in the enthronement of Jesus Christ. God declares the enthronement of His Son. The nations are incensed with bitter hatred against His cause. God is described as laughing at their enfeebled hate. The Lord "will laugh: the Lord will have them in derision"; "Yet I have set my king upon my holy hill of Zion" (Ps 2:4, 6). The decree has passed immutable and eternal:

> I will tell of the decree:
> Jehovah said unto me, Thou art my son;
> This day have I begotten thee.
> Ask of me, and I will give thee the nations for thine
>   inheritance,
> And the uttermost parts of the earth for thy posses-
>   sion.
> Thou shalt break them with a rod of iron;
> Thou shalt dash them in pieces like a potter's vessel.

PSALM 2:7-9

Ask of me is the condition—a praying people willing and obedient. "And men shall pray for him continually." Under this universal and simple promise men and women of old laid themselves out for God. They prayed and God answered their prayers, and the cause of God was kept alive in the world by the flame of their praying.

Prayer became a settled and only condition to move His Son's Kingdom. "Ask, and it shall be given you; seek, and ye shall find; knock, and it shall be opened" (Lk 11:9). The strongest one in Christ's Kingdom is he who is the best knocker. The secret of success in Christ's Kingdom is the ability to pray. The one who can wield the power of prayer is the strong one, the holy one in Christ's

Kingdom. The most important lesson we can learn is how to pray.

Prayer is the keynote of the most sanctified life, of the holiest ministry. He does the most for God who is the highest skilled in prayer. Jesus Christ exercised His ministry after this order.

We ought to give ourselves to God with regard to things both temporal and spiritual, and seek our satisfaction only in the fulfilling His will, whether He lead us by suffering, or by consolation, for all would be equal to a soul truly resigned. Prayer is nothing else but a sense of God's presence.

BROTHER LAWRENCE

Be sure you look to your secret duty; keep that up whatever you do. The soul cannot prosper in the neglect of it. Apostasy generally begins at the closet door. Be much in secret fellowship with God. It is secret trading that enriches the Christian.

Pray alone. Let prayer be the key of the morning and the bolt at night. The best way to fight against sin is to fight it on our knees.

PHILIP HENRY

An hour of solitude passed in sincere and earnest prayer, or the conflict with and conquest over a single passion or subtle bosom sin will teach us more of thought, will more effectually awaken the faculty and form the habit of reflection than a year's study in the schools without them.

COLERIDGE

2

POSSIBILITIES AND NECESSITY
OF PRAYER·

THE POSSIBILITIES and necessity of prayer, its power and
results are manifested in arresting and changing the purposes of God and in relieving the stroke of His power.
Abimelech was smitten by God:

> And Abraham prayed unto God: and God healed
> Abimelech, and his wife, and his maid-servants; and
> they bare *children*.
> For Jehovah had fast closed up all the wombs of
> the house of Abimelech, because of Sarah, Abra-
> ham's wife.
>
> GENESIS 20:17-18

Job's miserable, mistaken, comforters had so deported
themselves in their controversy with Job that God's wrath
was kindled against them. "My servant Job shall pray for
you," said God, "for him will I accept" (Job 42:8).

"And Jehovah turned the captivity of Job, when he
prayed for his friends" (v. 10).

Jonah was in dire condition when "Jehovah sent out
a great wind upon the sea, and there was a mighty tem-
pest" (Jon 1:4). When lots were cast, "the lot fell upon
Jonah" (v. 7). He was cast overboard into the sea, but
"Jehovah prepared a great fish to swallow up Jonah. . . .
Then Jonah prayed unto Jehovah his God out of the fish's

belly. . . . And Jehovah spake unto the fish, and it vomited out Jonah upon the dry land" (1:17—2:10) .

When the disobedient prophet lifted up his voice in prayer, God heard and sent deliverance.

Pharaoh was a firm believer in the possibilities of prayer and its ability to relieve. When staggering under the woeful curses of God, he pleaded with Moses to intercede for him. "Intreat Jehovah" (Ex 8:8) was his pathetic appeal four times repeated when the plagues were scourging Egypt. Four times were these urgent appeals made to Moses, and four times did prayer lift the dread curse from the hard king and his doomed land.

The blasphemy and idolatry of Israel in making the golden calf and declaring their devotion to it were fearful crimes. The anger of God waxed hot, and He declared that He would destroy the offending people. The Lord was very wroth with Aaron also, and to Moses He said, "Let me alone . . . that I may consume them" (Ex 32: 10) . But Moses prayed, and kept on praying; day and night he prayed forty days. He makes the record of his prayer struggle. "I fell down," he says, "before Jehovah, as at the first, forty days and forty nights; I did neither eat bread nor drink water; because of all your sin which ye sinned, in doing that which was evil in the sight of Jehovah, to provoke him to anger. For I was afraid of the anger and hot displeasure, wherewith Jehovah was wroth against you to destroy you. But Jehovah hearkened to me that time also. And Jehovah was very angry with Aaron to destroy him: and I prayed for Aaron also at the same time" (Deu 9:18-20) .

"Yet forty days, and Nineveh shall be overthrown" (Jon 1:3) . It was the purpose of God to destroy that great and wicked city. But Nineveh prayed, covered with sackcloth; sitting in ashes, she cried "mightily unto God" (Jon 3:8), and "God repented of the evil which he said he would do unto them; and he did it not" (v. 10).

The message of God to Hezekiah was "Set thine house in order; for thou shalt die, and not live" (Is 38:1). Hezekiah turned his face toward the wall, and prayed unto the Lord, and said: "Remember now, O Jehovah, I beseech thee, how I have walked before thee in truth and with a perfect heart, and have done that which is good in thy sight. And Hezekiah wept sore" (v. 3). God said to Isaiah, "Go, and say to Hezekiah, . . . I have heard thy prayer, I have seen thy tears; behold, I will add unto thy days fifteen years" (v. 5).

These men knew how to pray and how to prevail in prayer. Their faith in prayer was no passing attitude that changed with the wind or with their own feelings and circumstances; it was a fact that God heard and answered, that His ear was ever open to the cry of His children, and that the power to do what was asked of Him was commensurate with His willingness. And thus these men, strong in faith and in prayer, "subdued kingdoms, wrought righteousness, obtained promises, stopped the mouths of lions, quenched the power of fire, escaped the edge of the sword, from weakness were made strong, waxed mighty in war, turned to flight armies of the aliens" (Heb 11:33-34).

Everything then, as now, was possible to the men and women who knew how to pray. Prayer, indeed, opened a limitless storehouse, and God's hand withheld nothing. Prayer introduced those who practiced it into a world of privilege, and brought the strength and wealth of heaven down to the aid of finite man. What rich and wonderful power was theirs who had learned the secret of victorious

approach to God! With Moses it saved a nation; with
Ezra it saved a body of believers.

And yet, strange as it seems when we contemplate the
wonders of which God's people had been witness, there
came a slackness in prayer. The mighty hold upon God,
that had so often struck awe and terror into the heart of
their enemies, lost its grip. The people, backslidden and
apostate, had gone off from their praying, if the bulk of
them had ever truly prayed. The Pharisee's cold and lifeless praying was substituted for any genuine approach to
God; and because of that formal method of praying, the
whole worship became a parody of its real purpose. A
glorious dispensation, and gloriously executed was it by
Moses, by Ezra, by Daniel and Elijah, by Hannah and
Samuel; but the circle seems limited and short-lived; the
praying ones were few and far between. They had no sur-
vivors, none to imitate their devotion to God, none to
preserve the role of the elect.

In vain had the decree established the divine order, the
divine call. *Ask of Me.* From the earnest and fruitful
crying to God, they turned their faces to pagan gods and
cried in vain for the answers that could never come. And
so they sank into that godless and pitiful state that has lost
its object in life when the link with the eternal has been
broken. Their favored dispensation of prayer was forgotten; they knew not how to pray.

What a contrast to the achievements that brighten other pages of Holy Writ! The power working through
Elijah and Elisha in answer to prayer reached down even
to the very grave. In each case a child was raised from the
dead, and the powers of famine were broken. "The supplication of a righteous man availeth much" (Ja 5:16).
"Elijah was a man of like passions with us, and he prayed

fervently that it might not rain; and it rained not on the earth for three years and six months. And he prayed again; and the heaven gave rain, and the earth brought forth her fruit" (vv. 18-19). Jonah prayed while imprisoned in the great fish, and he came to dry land, saved from storm and sea and monsters of the deep by the mighty energy of his praying.

How wide the gracious provision of the grace of praying as administered in that marvelous dispensation! They prayed wondrously. Why could not their praying save the dispensation from decay and death? Was it not because they lost the fire without which all praying degenerates into a lifeless form? It takes effort and toil and care to prepare the incense. Prayer is no laggard's work. When all the rich, spiced graces from the body of prayer have by labor and beating been blended and refined and intermixed, the fire is needed to unloose the incense and make its fragrance rise to the throne of God. The fire that consumes creates the spirit and life of the incense. Without fire, prayer has no spirit; it is, like dead spices, for corruption and worms.

The casual, intermittent prayer is never bathed in this divine fire. For the man who thus prays is lacking in the earnestness that lays hold of God, determined not to let Him go until the blessing comes. "Pray without ceasing" (1 Th 5:17) counseled the great apostle. That is the habit that drives prayer right into the mortar that holds the building stones together. "You can do more than pray after you have prayed," said the godly Dr. A. J. Gordon, "but you cannot do more than pray until you have prayed." The story of every great Christian achievement is the history of answered prayer.

"The greatest and the best talent that God gives to any

man or woman in this world is the talent of prayer," writes Principal Alexander Whyte. "And the best usury that any man or woman brings back to God when He comes to reckon with them at the end of this world is a life of prayer. And those servants best put their Lord's money 'to the exchangers' who rise early and sit late, as long as they are in this world, ever finding out and ever following after better and better methods of prayer, and ever forming more secret, more steadfast, and more spiritually fruitful habits of prayer, till they literally 'pray without ceasing,' and till they continually strike out into new enterprises in prayer, and new achievements, and new enrichments."

Martin Luther, when once asked what his plans for the following day were, answered: "Work, work, from early until late. In fact, I have so much to do that I shall spend the first three hours in prayer." Cromwell, too, believed in being much upon his knees. Looking on one occasion at the statues of famous men, he turned to a friend and said, "Make mine kneeling, for thus I came to glory."

It is only when the whole heart is gripped with the passion of prayer that the life-giving fire descends, for none but the earnest man gets access to the ear of God.

When thou feelest thyself most indisposed to prayer yield not to it, but strive and endeavor to pray even when thou thinkest thou canst not pray.

HILDERSAM

It was among the Parthians the custom that none was to give their children any meat in the morning before they saw the sweat on their faces, and you shall find this to be

God's usual course not to give His children the taste of His delights till they begin to sweat in seeking after them.

RICHARD BAXTER

Of all the duties enjoined by Christianity none is more essential and yet more neglected than prayer. Most people consider the exercise a fatiguing ceremony, which they are justified in abridging as much as possible. Even those whose profession or fears lead them to pray, pray with such languor and wanderings of mind that their prayers, far from drawing down blessings, only increase their condemnation.

FENELON

The potency of prayer hath subdued the strength of fire; it had bridled the rage of lions, hushed anarchy to rest, extinguished wars, appeased the elements, expelled demons, burst the chains of death, expanded the gates of heaven, assuaged diseases, repelled frauds, rescued cities from destruction, stayed the sun in its course, and arrested the progress of the thunderbolt. Prayer is an all-efficient panoply, a treasure undiminished, a mine which is never exhausted, a sky unobscured by clouds, a heaven unruffled by the storm. It is the root, the fountain, the mother of a thousand blessings.

CHRYSOSTOM

3

MORE AND BETTER PRAYING
THE SECRET OF SUCCESS

More praying and better is the secret of the whole matter. More time for prayer, more relish and preparation to meet God, to commune with God through Christ—this has in it the whole of the matter. Our manner and matter of praying ill become us. The attitude and relationship of God and the Son are the eternal relationship of Father and Son, of asking and giving—the Son always asking, the Father always giving:

> Ask of me, and I will give thee the nations for thine inheritance,
> And the uttermost parts of the earth for thy possession.
> Thou shalt break them with a rod of iron;
> Thou shalt dash them in pieces like a potter's vessel.

> PSALM 2:8-9

Jesus is to be always praying through His people. "For my house shall be called a house of prayer for all peoples" (Is 56:7). We must prepare ourselves to pray, to be like Christ, to pray like Christ.

Man's access in prayer to God opens everything and makes his impoverishment his wealth. All things are his through prayer. The wealth and the glory—all things are Christ's. As the light grows brighter and prophets take in the nature of the restoration, the divine record seems to be enlarged. "Thus saith Jehovah, the Holy One of Israel, and his Maker; Ask me of the things that are to come: concerning my sons, and concerning the work of my hands, command ye me. I have made the earth, and created man upon it: I, even my hands, have stretched out the heavens; and all their host have I commanded" (Is 45:11-12).

To man is given to command God with all this authority and power in the demands of God's earthly Kingdom. Heaven, with all it has, is under tribute to carry out the ultimate, final, and glorious purposes of God. Why then is the time so long in carrying out these wise benedictions for man? Why then does sin reign so long? Why are the oath-bound covenant promises so long in coming to their gracious end? Sin reigns, Satan reigns, sighing marks the lives of many; all tears are fresh and full.

Why is all this so? We have not prayed to bring the evil to an end; we have not prayed as we must pray. We have not met the conditions of prayer.

Ask of me. Ask of God. We have not rested on prayer. We have not made prayer the sole condition. There has been violation of the primary condition of prayer. We have not prayed aright. We have not prayed at all. God is willing to give, but we are slow to ask. The Son, through His saints, is ever praying, and God the Father is ever answering.

Ask of me. In the invitation is conveyed the assurance of answer; the shout of victory is there and may be heard by the listening ear. The Father holds the authority and power in His hands. How easy is the condition, and yet how long are we in fulfilling the conditions! Nations are in bondage; the uttermost parts of the earth are still unpossessed. The earth groans; the world is still in bondage; Satan and evil hold sway.

The Father holds Himself in the attitude of Giver, *Ask of me,* and that petition to God the Father empowers all agencies, inspires all movements. The Gospel is divinely inspired. Back of all its inspirations is prayer. *Ask of me* lies back of all movements. Standing as the endowment of the enthroned Christ is the oath-bound covenant of the Father, "Ask of me, and I will give thee the nations for thine inheritance, and the uttermost parts of the earth for thy possession.

Ever are the prayers of holy men streaming up to God as fragrant as the richest incense. And God in many ways is speaking to us, declaring His wealth and our impoverishment: "The earth is the LORD's and the fulness thereof" (Ps 24:1, KJV).

We can do all things by God's aid, and can have the whole of His aid by asking. The Gospel, in its success and power, depends on our ability to pray. The dispensations of God depend on man's ability to pray. We can have all that God has. *Command ye me.* This is no figment of the imagination, no idle dream, no vain fancy. The life of the Church is the highest life. Its office is to pray. Its prayer life is the highest life, the most odorous, the most conspicuous.

The book of Revelation says nothing about prayer as a great duty, a hallowed service, but much about prayer in its aggregated force and energies. It is the prayer force ever living and ever praying; it is all saints' prayers going out as a mighty, living energy while the lips that uttered the words are stilled and sealed in death, while the living Church has an energy of faith to inherit the forces of all the past praying and make it deathless.

The statement by the Baptist philosopher, John Foster, contains the purest philosophy and the simple truth of God, for God has no force and demands no conditions but prayer. "More and better praying will bring the surest and readiest triumph to God's cause; feeble, formal, listless praying brings decay and death. The Church has its sheet-anchor in the closet; its magazine stores are there."

"I am convinced," Foster continues, "that every man who amidst his serious projects is apprized of his dependence upon God as completely as that dependence is a fact, will be impelled to pray and be anxious to induce his serious friends to pray almost every hour. He will not without it promise himself any noble success any more than a mariner would expect to reach a distant coast by having his sails spread in a stagnation of air.

"I have intimated my fear that it is visionary to expect an unusual success in the human administration of religion unless there are unusual omens: now a most emphatical spirit of prayer would be such an omen; and the individual who should determine to try its last possible efficacy might probably find himself becoming a much more prevailing agent in his little sphere. And if the whole, or the greater number of the disciples of Christianity were with an earnest and unalterable resolution of each to combine that heaven should not withhold one single influence which the very utmost effort of conspiring and persevering supplication would obtain, it would be a sign that a revolution of the world was at hand."

Edward Payson, one of God's own, says of this statement of Foster, "Very few missionaries since the apostles, probably, have tried the experiment. He who shall make the first trial will, I believe, effect wonders. Nothing that I could write, nothing that an angel could write, would be necessary to him who should make this trial.

"One of the principal results of the little experience which I have had as a Christian minister is a conviction that religion consists very much in giving God that place in our views and feelings which He actually fills in the universe. We know that in the universe He is all in all. So far as He is constantly all in all to us, so far as we comply with the Psalmist's charge to his soul, 'My soul, wait thou *only* upon God'; so far, I apprehend, have we advanced towards perfection. It is comparatively easy to wait upon God; but to wait upon Him *only*—to feel, so far as our strength, happiness, and usefulness are concerned, as if all creatures and second causes were annihilated, and we were alone in the universe with God, is, I suspect, a difficult and rare attainment. At least, I am sure it is one which I am very far from having made. In proportion as we make this attainment we shall find everything easy; for we shall become, emphatically, men of prayer; and we may say of prayer as Solomon says of money, that it answereth all things."

This same John Foster said, when approaching death: "I never prayed more earnestly nor probably with such faithful frequency. 'Pray without ceasing' has been the sentence repeating itself in the silent thought, and I am sure it must be my practice till the last conscious hour of life. Oh, why not throughout that long, indolent, inanimate half-century past?"

And yet this is the way in which we all act about prayer. Conscious as we are of its importance, of its vital importance, we yet let the hours pass away as a blank and can only lament in death the irremediable loss.

When we calmly reflect upon the fact that the progress

of our Lord's Kingdom is dependent upon prayer, it is sad to think that we give so little time to the holy exercise. Everything depends upon prayer, and yet we neglect it not only to our own spiritual hurt but also to the delay and injury of our Lord's cause upon earth. The forces of good and evil are contending for the world. If we would, we could add to the conquering power of the army of righteousness, and yet our lips are sealed, our hands hang listlessly by our side, and we jeopardize the very cause in which we profess to be deeply interested by holding back from the prayer chamber.

Prayer is the one prime, eternal condition by which the Father is pledged to put the Son in possession of the world. Christ prays through His people. Had there been importunate, universal, and continuous prayer by God's people, long ere this the earth had been possessed for Christ. The delay is not to be accounted for by the inveterate obstacles, but by the lack of the right asking. We do more of everything else than of praying. As poor as our giving is, our contributions of money exceed our offerings of prayer. Perhaps in the average congregation fifty aid in paying, where one saintly, ardent soul shuts himself up with God and wrestles for the deliverance of the heathen world. Official praying on set or state occasions counts for nothing in this estimate. We emphasize other things more than we do the necessity of prayer.

We are saying prayers after an orderly way, but we have not the world in the grasp of our faith. We are not praying after the order that moves God and brings all divine influences to help us. The world needs more true praying to save it from the reign and ruin of Satan.

We do not pray as Elijah prayed. John Foster puts the whole matter to a practical point. "When the Church of

God," he says, "is aroused to its obligation and duties
and right faith to claim what Christ has promised—'all
things whatsoever'—a revolution will take place."

But not all praying is praying. The driving power, the
conquering force, in God's cause is God Himself. "Call
unto me, and I will answer thee, and show thee great
things, and difficult, which thou knowest not" (Jer 33:3)
is God's challenge to prayer. Prayer puts God in full force
into God's work. "Ask me of the things that are to come:
concerning my sons, and concerning the work of my
hands, command ye me"—God's carte blanche to prayer.
Faith is only omnipotent when on its knees, and its out-
stretched hands take hold of God, then it draws to the utmost of God's capacity; for only a praying faith can get
God's "all things whatsoever." Wonderful lessons are the
Syrophenician woman, the importunate widow, and the
friend at midnight, of what dauntless prayer can do in
mastering or defying conditions, in changing defeat into
victory and triumphing in the regions of despair. One-
ness with Christ, the acme of spiritual attainment, is
glorious in all things; most glorious in that we can then
ask what we will and it shall be done unto us. Prayer in
Jesus' name puts the crowning crown on God, because it
glorifies Him through the Son and pledges the Son to give
to men whatsoever and anything they shall ask.

In the New Testament the marvelous prayer of the Old
Testament is put to the front that it may provoke and
stimulate our praying, and it is preceded with a declaration, the dynamic energy of which we can scarcely trans-
late. "The supplication of a righteous man availeth much
in its working. Elijah was a man of like passions with us,
and he prayed fervently that it might not rain; and it
rained not on the earth for three years and six months.

And he prayed again; and the heaven gave rain, and the earth brought forth her fruit" (Ja 5:17-19).

Our paucity in results, the cause of all leanness, is solved by the apostle James: "Ye have not, because ye ask not. Ye ask, and receive not, because ye ask amiss, that ye may spend it on your pleasures" (Ja 4:2-3).

That is the whole truth in a nutshell.

I never prayed sincerely and earnestly for anything but it came at some time—no matter at how distant a day, somehow, in some shape, probably the last I would have devised, it came.

ADONIRAM JUDSON

4

INCIDENTS OF MIGHTY PRAYER

IT WAS SAID of the late C. H. Spurgeon that he glided from laughter to prayer with the naturalness of one who lived in both elements. With him the habit of prayer was free and unfettered. His life was not divided into compartments, the one shut off from the other with a rigid exclusiveness that barred all intercommunication. He lived in constant fellowship with his Father in heaven. He was ever in touch with God, and thus it was as natural for him to pray as it was for him to breathe.

"What a fine time we have had; let us thank God for it," he said to a friend on one occasion, when, out under the blue sky and wrapped in glorious sunshine, they had enjoyed a holiday with the unfettered enthusiasm of schoolboys. Prayer sprang as spontaneously to his lips as did ordinary speech, and never was there the slightest incongruity in his approach to the divine throne straight from any scene in which he might be taking part.

That is the attitude with regard to prayer that ought to mark every child of God. There are, and there ought to be, stated seasons of communion with God when, everything else shut out, we come into His presence to talk to Him and to let Him speak to us; and out of such seasons springs that beautiful habit of prayer that weaves a golden bond between earth and heaven. Without such stated seasons the habit of prayer can never be formed; without them there is no nourishment for the spiritual life. By means of them the soul is lifted into a new atmosphere, the atmosphere of the heavenly city in which it is easy to open the heart to God and to speak with Him as friend speaks with friend.

Thus, in every circumstance of life, prayer is the most natural outpouring of the soul, the unhindered turning to God for communion and direction. Whether in sorrow or in joy, in defeat or in victory, in health or in weakness, in calamity or in success, the heart leaps to meet God just as a child runs to his mother's arms, ever sure that with her is the sympathy that meets every need.

Dr. Adam Clarke, in his autobiography, records that when Mr. Wesley was returning to England by ship, considerable delay was caused by contrary winds. Wesley was reading when he became aware of some confusion on board. Asking what was the matter, he was informed that the wind was contrary. "Then," was his reply, "let us go to prayer."

After Dr. Clarke had prayed, Wesley broke out into fervent supplication which seemed to be more the offering of faith than of mere desire. "Almighty and everlasting God," he prayed, "Thou hast sway everywhere, and all things serve the purpose of Thy will; Thou holdest the winds in Thy fists and sittest upon the water floods, and reignest a King forever. Command these winds and these waves that they obey Thee, and take us speedily and safely to the haven whither we would go."

The power of this petition was felt by all. Wesley rose from his knees, made no remark, but took up his book and continued reading. Dr. Clarke went on deck and, to his surprise, found the vessel under sail, standing on her right course. Nor did she change till she was safely at anchor. On the sudden and favorable change of wind, Wesley made no remark; so fully did he expect to be heard that he took it for granted that he was heard.

That was prayer with a purpose—the definite and direct utterance of one who knew that he had the ear of God, and that God had the willingness as well as the power to grant the petition which he asked of Him.

Major D. W. Whittle, in an introduction to the wonders of prayer, says of George Mueller of Bristol: "I met Mr. Mueller in the express, the morning of our sailing from Quebec to Liverpool. About half an hour before the tender was to take the passengers to the ship, he asked of the agent if a deck chair had arrived for him from New York. He was answered, 'No,' and told that it could not possibly come in time for the steamer. I had with me a chair I had just purchased, and told Mr. Mueller of the place nearby, and suggested, as but a few moments remained that he had better buy one at once. His reply was, 'No, my brother. Our heavenly Father will send the chair from New York. It is one used by Mrs. Mueller. I wrote ten days ago to a brother, who promised to see it forwarded here last week. He has not been prompt, as I would have desired, but I am sure our heavenly Father will send the chair. Mrs. Mueller is very sick on the sea, and has particularly desired to have this same chair, and not finding it here yesterday, we have made special prayer that our heavenly Father would be pleased to provide it for us, and we will trust Him to do so.' As this dear man of God went peacefully on board, running the risk of Mrs. Mueller making the trip without a chair, when, for a couple of dollars, she could have been provided for, I confess I feared Mr. Mueller was carrying his faith principles too far and not acting wisely. I was kept at the express office ten minutes after Mr. Mueller left. Just as I started to hurry to the wharf, a team drove up the street, and on top of a load just arrived from New York was *Mr. Mueller's chair.* It was sent at once to the tender and placed in *my hands* to take to Mr. Mueller, just as the boat was leaving the dock (the Lord having a lesson for me). Mr. Mueller took it with the happy, pleased expression of a child who has just received a kindness deeply appreciated and reverently removing his hat and folding his hands over it, he thanked the heavenly Father for sending the chair."

One of Melancthon's correspondents writes of Luther's praying: "I cannot enough admire the extraordinary cheerfulness, constancy, faith and hope of the man in these trying and vexatious times. He constantly feeds these gracious affections by a very diligent study of the Word of God. *Then not a day passes in which he does not employ in prayer at least three of his very best hours.* Once I happened to hear him at prayer. Gracious God! What spirit and what faith is there in his expressions! He petitions God with as much reverence as if he was in the divine presence, and yet with as firm a hope and confidence as he would address a father or a friend. 'I know,' said he, 'Thou art our Father and our God; and therefore I am sure Thou wilt bring to naught the persecutors of Thy children. For shouldest Thou fail to do this, Thine own cause, being connected with ours, would be endangered. It is entirely Thine own concern. We, by Thy providence, have been compelled to take a part. Thou therefore wilt be our defense.' Whilst I was listening to Luther praying in this manner, at a distance, my soul seemed on fire within me, to hear the man address God so like a friend, yet with so much gravity and reverence; and also to hear him, in the course of his prayer, insisting on the promises contained in the Psalms, as if he were sure his petitions would be granted."

Of William Bramwell, a noted Methodist preacher in England, wonderful for his zeal and prayer, the following is related by a sergeant major: "In July, 1811, our regiment was ordered for Spain, then the seat of a protracted and sanguinary war. My mind was painfully exercised with the thoughts of leaving my dear wife and four helpless children in a strange country, unprotected and unprovided for. Mr. Bramwell felt a lively interest in our situation, and his sympathizing spirit seemed to drink in all the agonized feelings of my tender wife. He supplicated the throne of grace day and night in our behalf. My wife and I spent the evening previous to our march at a friend's house, in company with Mr. Bramwell who sat in a very pensive mood, and appeared to be in a spiritual struggle all the time. After supper, he suddenly pulled his hand out of his bosom, laid it on my knee, and said: 'Brother Riley, mark what I am about to say! You are not to go to Spain. Remember, I tell you, you are not; for I have been wrestling with God on your behalf, and when my Heavenly Father condescends in mercy to bless me with power to lay hold on Himself, I do not easily let Him go; no, not until I am favoured with an answer. Therefore you may depend upon it that the next time I hear from you, you will be settled in quarters.' This came to pass exactly as he said. The next day the order for going to Spain was countermanded."

These men prayed with a purpose. To them God was not far away, in some inaccessible region, but near at hand, ever ready to listen to the call of His children. There was no barrier between. They were on terms of perfect intimacy, if one may use such a phrase in relation to man and his Maker. No cloud obscured the face of the Father from His trusting child, who could look up into the divine countenance and pour out the longings of his heart. And that is the type of prayer which God never fails to hear. He knows that it comes from a heart at one with His own, from one who is entirely yielded to the heavenly plan, and so He bends His ear and gives to the pleading child the assurance that his petition has been heard and answered.

Have we not all had some such experience when with set and undeviating purpose we have approached the face of our Father? In an agony of soul we have sought refuge from the oppression of the world in the anteroom of heaven; the waves of despair seemed to threaten destruction, and as no way of escape was visible anywhere, we fell back, like the disciples of old, upon the power of our Lord, crying to Him to save us lest we perish. And then, in the twinkling of an eye, the thing was done. The billows sank into a calm; the howling wind died down at the divine command; the agony of the soul passed into a restful peace as over the whole being there crept the consciousness of the divine presence, bringing with it the assurance of answered prayer and sweet deliverance.

"I tell the Lord my troubles and difficulties, and wait for Him to give me the answers to them," says one man of God. "And it is wonderful how a matter that looked very dark will in prayer become clear as crystal by the help of God's Spirit. I think Christians fail so often to get answers to their prayers because they do not wait long enough on God. They just drop down and say a few words, and then jump up and forget it and expect God to answer them. Such praying always reminds me of the small boy ringing his neighbor's doorbell, and then running away as fast as he can go."

When we acquire the habit of prayer we enter into a new atmosphere. "Do you expect to go to heaven?" asked someone of a devout Scotsman. "Why, man, I live there!" was the quaint and unexpected reply. It was a pithy statement of a great truth, for all the way to heaven is heaven begun to the Christian who walks near enough to God to hear the secrets He has to impart.

This attitude is beautifully illustrated in a story of Horace Bushnell, told by Dr. Parkes Cadman. Bushnell was found to be suffering from an incurable disease. One evening the Reverend Joseph Twichell visited him; as they sat together under the starry sky, Bushnell said, "One of us ought to pray." Twichell asked Bushnell to do so, and Bushnell began his prayer; burying his face in the earth, he poured out his heart until, said Twichell, in recalling the incident, "I was afraid to stretch out my hand in the darkness lest I should touch God."

To have God thus near is to enter the holy of holies, to breathe the fragrance of the heavenly air, to walk in Eden's delightful gardens. Nothing but prayer can bring God and man into this happy communion. That was the experience of everyone who passes through the same gateway. When this saint of God was confined in jail at one time for conscience's sake, he enjoyed in a rare degree the divine companionship, recording in his diary that Jesus entered his cell, and that at His coming "every stone flashed like a ruby."

Many others have borne witness to the same sweet fellowship, when prayer had become the one habit of life that meant more than anything else to them. David Livingstone lived in the realm of prayer and knew its gracious influence. It was his habit every birthday to write a prayer, and on the next to the last birthday of all, this was his prayer: "O Divine One, I have not loved Thee earnestly, deeply, sincerely enough. Grant, I pray Thee, that before this year is ended I may have finished my task." It was just on the threshold of the year that followed that his faithful men, as they looked into the hut of Ilala, while the rain dripped from the eaves, saw their master on his knees beside his bed in an attitude of prayer. He had died on his knees in prayer.

Stonewall Jackson was a man of prayer. Said he: "I have so fixed the habit in my mind that I never raise a glass of water to my lips without asking God's blessing, never seal a letter without putting a word of prayer under the seal, never take a letter from the post without a brief sending of my thoughts heavenward, never change my classes in the lecture room without a minute's petition for the cadets who go out and for those who come in."

James Gilmour, the pioneer missionary to Mongolia, was a man of prayer. He had a habit in his writing of never using a blotter. He made a rule when he got to the bottom of any page to wait until the ink dried and spend the time in prayer.

In this way their whole being was saturated with the divine, and they became the reflectors of the heavenly fragrance and glory. Walking with God down the avenues of prayer we acquire something of His likeness, and unconsciously we become witnesses to others of His beauty and His grace. Professor James in his famous work, *Varieties of Religious Experience,* tells of a man of forty-nine who said: "God is more real to me than any thought or thing or person. I feel His presence positively, and the more as I live in closer harmony with His laws as written in my body and mind. I feel Him in the sunshine or rain; and all mingled with a delicious restfulness most nearly describes my feelings. I talk to Him as to a companion in prayer and praise, and our communion is delightful. He answers me again and again, often in words so clearly spoken that it seems my outer ear must have carried the tone, but generally in strong mental impressions. Usually a text of Scripture, unfolding some new view of Him and His love for me, and care for my safety. . . . That He is mine and I am His never leaves me; it is an abiding joy. Without it life would be a blank, a desert, a shoreless, trackless waste."

Equally notable is the testimony of Sir Thomas Browne, the beloved physician who lived at Norwich in 1605, and was the author of a very remarkable book of wide circulation, *Religio Medici*. In spite of the fact that England was passing through a period of national convulsion and political excitement, he found comfort and strength in prayer. "I have resolved," he wrote in a journal found among his private papers after his death, "to pray more and pray always, to pray in all places where quietness inviteth, in the house, on the highway and on the street; and to know no street or passage in this city that may not witness that I have not forgotten God." And he adds: "I purpose to take occasion of praying upon the sight of any church which I may pass, that God may be worshipped there in spirit, and that souls may be saved there; to pray daily for my sick patients and for the patients of other physicians; at my entrance into any home to say, 'May the peace of God abide here'; after hearing a sermon, to pray for a blessing on God's truth, and upon the messenger; upon the sight of a beautiful person to bless God for His creatures, to pray for the beauty of such an one's soul, that God may enrich her with inward graces, and that the outward and inward may correspond; upon the sight of a deformed person, to pray to God to give them wholeness of soul, and by-and-by to give them the beauty of the resurrection."

What an illustration of the praying spirit! Such an attitude represents prayer without ceasing, reveals the habit of prayer in its unceasing supplication, in its uninterrupted communion, in its constant intercession. What an illustration, too, of purpose in prayer! Of how many of us can it be said that as we pass people in the street we pray for them, or that as we enter a home or a church we remember the inhabitants or the congregation in prayer to God?

The explanation of our thoughtlessness or forgetfulness lies in the fact that prayer with so many of us is simply a form of selfishness; it means asking for something for ourselves—that and nothing more.

And from such an attitude we need to pray to be delivered.

The prayer of faith is the only power in the universe to which the great Jehovah yields. Prayer is the sovereign remedy.

ROBERT HALL

The Church, intent on the acquisition of temporal power, had well-nigh abandoned its spiritual duties, and its empire, which rested on spiritual foundations, was crumbling with their decay, and threatened to pass away like an unsubstantial vision.

LEA'S INQUISITION

Let me burn out for God. After all, whatever God may appoint, prayer is the great thing. Oh, that I may be a man of prayer.

HENRY MARTYN

5

NO SUBSTITUTE FOR PRAYER

ARE WE PRAYING as Christ did? Do we abide in Him? Are our pleas and spirit the overflow of His spirit and pleas? Does love—perfect love—rule the spirit?

These questions must be considered as proper and apposite at a time like the present. We do fear that we are doing more of other things than prayer. This is not a praying age; it is an age of great activity, of great movements, but one in which the tendency is very strong to stress the seen and the material and to neglect and discount the unseen and the spiritual. Prayer is the greatest of all forces because it honors God and brings Him into active aid.

There can be no substitute, no rival for prayer; it stands alone as the great spiritual force, and this force must be imminent and acting. It cannot be dispensed with during one generation, nor held in abeyance for the advance of any great movement. It must be continuous and particular, always, everywhere, and in everything. We cannot run our spiritual operations on the prayers of the past generation. *Many persons believe in the efficacy of prayer, but not many pray.* Prayer is the easiest and hardest of all things; the simplest and the sublimest; the weakest and the most powerful; its results lie outside the range of human possibilities; they are limited only by the omnipotence of God.

Few Christians have anything but a vague idea of the power of prayer; fewer still have any experience of that power. The Church seems almost wholly unaware of the power God puts into her hand; this spiritual carte blanche on the infinite resources of God's wisdom and power is rarely, if ever, used, and it is never used to the full measure of honoring God. It is astounding how poor the use, how little the benefits. Prayer is our most formidable weapon, but the one in which we are the least skilled, the most averse to its use. We do everything else for the heathen except the things God wants us to do; prayer is the only thing which does any good and makes all else we do efficient.

To graduate in the school of prayer is to master the whole course of a religious life. The first and last stages of holy living are crowned with praying. It is a life trade. The hindrances of prayer are the hindrances in a holy life. The conditions of praying are the conditions of righteousness, holiness, and salvation. A cobbler in the trade of praying is a bungler in the trade of salvation.

Prayer is a trade to be learned. We must be apprentices and serve our time at it. Painstaking care, much thought, practice, and labor are required to be a skillful tradesman in praying. Practice in this, as well as in all other trades makes perfect. Only toiling hands and hearts make people proficient in this heavenly trade.

In spite of the benefits and blessings which flow from communion with God, the sad confession must be made that we are not praying much. A very small number comparatively lead in prayer at the meetings. Fewer still pray with their families. Fewer still are in the habit of praying regularly in their closets. Meetings specially for prayer are as rare as frost in June. In many churches there is neither the name nor the semblance of a prayer meeting. In the town and city churches the prayer meeting in name is not a prayer meeting in fact. A sermon or a lecture is the main feature. Prayer is the nominal attachment.

Our people are not essentially a praying people. That is evident by their lives.

Prayer and a holy life are one. They mutually act and react. Neither can survive alone. The absence of the one is the absence of the other. The monk substituted superstition for praying; therefore, mummeries and routine took the place of a holy life. We are in danger of substituting churchly work and a ceaseless round of showy activities for prayer and holy living. A holy life does not live in the closet, but it cannot live without the closet. If, by any chance, a prayer chamber should be established without a holy life, it would be a chamber without the presence of God in it.

To put saints everywhere to praying is the burden of the apostolic effort and the keynote of apostolic success. Jesus Christ had striven to do this in the days of His personal ministry. He was moved by infinite compassion at the ripened fields of earth perishing for lack of laborers, and pausing in His own praying, He tries to awaken the sleeping sensibilities of His disciples to the duty of prayer, as He charges them: "Pray ye therefore the Lord of the harvest, that he send forth laborers into his harvest" (Mt 9:38). And He spake a parable to them to this end, that men ought always to pray.

Only glimpses of this great importance of prayer could the apostles receive before Pentecost. But the Spirit coming and filling on Pentecost elevated prayer to its vital and all-commanding position in the Gospel of Christ. The call now of prayer to every saint is the Spirit's loudest and most exigent call. Sainthood's piety is made, refined, perfected, by prayer. The Gospel moves with slow and timid pace when the saints are not at their prayers early and late and long.

Where are the Christ-like leaders who can teach the modern saints how to pray and put them at it? Do our leaders know we are raising up a prayerless set of saints? Where are the apostolic leaders who can put God's people to praying? Let them come to the front and do the work, and it will be the greatest work that can be done. An increase of educational facilities and a great increase of money force will be the direst curse to religion if they are not sanctified by more and better praying than we are doing.

More praying will not come as a matter of course. The campaign for the twentieth or thirtieth century will not help our praying, but hinder if we are not careful. Nothing but a specific effort from a praying leadership will avail. None but praying leaders can have praying followers. Praying apostles will beget praying saints. A praying pulpit will beget praying pews. We do greatly need somebody who can set the saints to this business of praying. We are a generation of nonpraying saints. Nonpraying saints are a beggarly gang of saints who have neither the ardor nor the beauty nor the power of saints. Who will restore this branch? The greatest will he be of reformers and apostles who can set the Church to praying.

Holy men have, in the past, changed the whole force of affairs, revolutionized character and country by prayer. And such achievements are still possible to us. The power is only wanting to be used. Prayer is but the expression of faith.

shall not God avenge his elect, which cry to him day and night, and he is long-suffering over them? I say unto you, that he will avenge them speedily. Nevertheless, when the Son of man cometh, shall he find faith on the earth?" (Lk 18:1-8) .

This poor woman's case was a most hopeless one, but importunity brings hope from the realms of despair and creates success where neither success nor its conditions existed. There could be no stronger case to show how unwearied and dauntless importunity gains its ends where everything else fails. The preface to this parable says: He spake a parable . . . to the end that they ought always to pray, and not to faint." He knew that men would soon get fainthearted in praying, so to hearten us He gives this picture of the marvelous power of importunity.

The widow, weak and helpless, is helplessness personed; bereft of every hope and influence which could move an unjust judge, she yet wins her case solely by her tireless and aggressive importunity. Could the necessity of importunity, its power and tremendous importance in prayer, be pictured in deeper or more impressive coloring? It surmounts or removes all obstacles, overcomes every resisting force, and gains its ends in the face of invincible hindrances. We can do nothing without prayer. All things can be done by importunate prayer.

That is the teaching of Jesus Christ.

Another parable spoken by Jesus enforces the same great truth. A man at midnight goes to his friend for a loaf of bread. His pleas are strong, based on friendship and the embarrassing and exacting demands of necessity, but these all fail. He gets no bread, but he stays and pleases, and waits and gains. Sheer importunity succeeds where all other pleas and influences had failed.

Time would fail to tell of the mighty things wrought by prayer, for by it holy ones have "subdued kingdoms, wrought righteousness, obtained promises, stopped the mouths of lions, quenched the power of fire, escaped the edge of the sword, from weakness were made strong, waxed mighty in war, turned to flight armies of aliens. Women received their dead by a resurrection" (Heb 11:33-35) .

Prayer honors God; it dishonors self. It is man's plea of weakness, ignorance, want, a plea which heaven cannot disregard. God delights to have us pray.

Prayer is not the foe to work; it does not paralyze activity. It works mightily; prayer itself is the greatest work. It springs activity, stimulates desire and effort. Prayer is not an opiate but a tonic; it does not lull to sleep but arouses anew for action. The lazy man does not, will not, cannot pray, for prayer demands energy. Paul calls it a striving, an agony. With Jacob it was a wrestling; with the Syrophoenician woman it was a struggle which called into play all the higher qualities of the soul, and which demanded great force to meet.

The closet is not an asylum for the indolent and worthless Christian. It is not a nursery where none but babes belong. It is the battlefield of the Church, its citadel, the scene of heroic and unearthly conflicts. The closet is the base of supplies for the Christian and the Church. Cut off from it there is nothing left but retreat and disaster. The energy for work, the mastery over self, the deliverance from fear, all spiritual results and graces, are much advanced by prayer. The difference between the strength, the experience, the holiness of Christians is found in the contrast in their praying.

Few, short, and feeble prayers betoken a low spiritual

condition. Men ought to pray much and to apply themselves to it with energy and perseverance. Eminent Christians have been eminent in prayer. The deep things of
God are learned nowhere else. Great things for God are
done by great prayers. He who prays much, studies much,
loves much, and works much does much for God and
humanity. The execution of the Gospel, the vigor of
faith, the maturity and excellence of spiritual graces wait
on prayer.

*"Nothing is impossible to industry," said one of the
seven sages of Greece. Let us change the word industry
for persevering prayer, and the motto will be more
Christian and more worthy of universal adoption. I am
persuaded that we are all more deficient in a spirit of
prayer than in any other grace. God loves importunate
prayer so much that He will not give us much blessing
without it. And the reason that He loves such prayer is
that He loves us and knows that it is a necessary preparation for our receiving the richest blessings which He is
waiting and longing to bestow.*

6

IMPORTUNITY: CHARACTERIS
OF REAL PRAYER

CHRIST PUTS IMPORTUNITY as a distinguishing cha
tic of true praying. We must not only pray, but
pray with great urgency, with intentness, and wit
tion. We must not only pray, but we must pray a
again. We must not get tired of praying. We
thoroughly in earnest, deeply concerned about t
for which we ask, for Jesus Christ made it very
the secret of prayer and its success lie in its urg
must press our prayers upon God.

In a parable of exquisite pathos and simp
Lord taught not simply that men ought to pra
men ought to pray with full heartiness, an
matter with vigorous energy and brave hearts

"And he spake a parable unto them to t
they ought always to pray, and not to faint; s
was in a city a judge, which feared not God, a
not man: and there was a widow in that
came oft unto him, saying, Avenge me of m
And he would not for a while: but after
within himself, Though I fear not God, no
yet because this widow troubleth me, I w
lest she wear me out by her continual con
Lord said, Hear what the unrighteous ju

The case of the Syrophoenician woman is a parable in action. She is arrested in her approaches to Christ by the information that He will not see anyone. She is denied His presence, and then in His presence is treated with seeming indifference, with the chill of silence and unconcern. She presses and approaches, the pressure and approach are repulsed by the stern and crushing statement that He is not sent to her kith or kind, that she is reprobated from His mission and power. She is humiliated by being called a dog. Yet she accepts all, overcomes all, wins all by her humble, dauntless, invincible importunity. The Son of God, pleased, surprised, overpowered by her unconquerable importunity, says to her: "O woman, great is thy faith: be it done unto thee even as thou wilt" (Mt 15:28). Jesus Christ surrenders Himself to the importunity of a great faith. "And shall not God avenge his own elect, that cry to him day and night, and yet he is longsuffering over them?" (Lk 18:7).

Jesus Christ puts the ability to importune as one of the elements of prayer, one of the main conditions of prayer. The prayer of the Syrophoenician woman is an exhibition of the matchless power of importunity, of a conflict more real and involving more of vital energy, endurance, and all the higher elements than was ever illustrated in the conflicts of Isthmia or Olympia.

The first lessons of importunity are taught in the Sermon on the Mount, "Ask, and it shall be given you; seek, and ye shall find; knock, and it shall be opened" (Mt 7:7). These are steps of advance: "For every one that asketh receiveth; and he that seeketh findeth; and to him that knocketh it shall be opened" (v. 8).

Without continuance the prayer may go unanswered. Importunity is made up of the ability to hold on, to press

on, to wait with unrelaxed and unrelaxable grasp, rest-
less desire, and restful patience. Importunate prayer is
not an incident but the main thing, not a performance
but a passion, not a need but a necessity.

Prayer in its highest form and grandest success assumes
the attitude of a wrestler with God. It is the contest, trial,
and victory of faith; a victory not secured from an enemy,
but from Him who tries our faith that He may enlarge
it, who tests our strength to make us stronger. Few things
give such quickened and permanent vigor to the soul as a
long exhaustive season of importunate prayer. It makes
an experience, an epoch, a new calendar for the spirit, a
new life to religion, a soldierly training. The Bible never
wearies in its pressure and illustration of the fact that the
highest spiritual good is secured as the return of the out-
going of the highest form of spiritual effort. There is
neither encouragement nor room in Bible religion for
feeble desires, listless efforts, lazy attitudes; all must be
strenuous, urgent, ardent. Inflamed desires, impassioned,
unwearied insistence delight heaven. God would have
His children incorrigibly in earnest and persistently bold
in their efforts. Heaven is too busy to listen to halfhearted
prayers.

Our whole being must be in our praying; like John
Knox, we must say and feel, "Give me Scotland, or I die."
Our experience and revelations of God are born of our
costly sacrifice, our costly conflicts, our costly praying.
The wrestling, all-night praying of Jacob made an era
never to be forgotten in Jacob's life, brought God to the
rescue, changed Esau's attitude and conduct, changed
Jacob's character, saved and affected his life, and entered
into the habits of a nation.

Our seasons of importunate prayer cut themselves, like

the print of a diamond, into our hardest places, and mark with ineffaceable traces our characters. They are the salient periods of our lives, the memorial stones which endure and to which we turn.

Importunity, it may be repeated, is a condition of prayer. We are to press the matter, not with vain repetitions, but with urgent repetitions. We repeat, not to count the times, but to gain the prayer. We cannot quit praying, because heart and soul are in it. We pray "in all perseverance" (Eph 6:18). We hang on to our prayers because by them we live. We press our pleas because we must have them or die. Christ gives us two most expressive parables to emphasize the necessity of importunity in praying. Perhaps Abraham lost Sodom by failing to press to the utmost his privilege of praying. Joash, we know, lost because he stayed his smiting.

Perseverance counts much with God as well as with man. If Elijah had ceased at his first petition, the heavens would have scarcely yielded their rain to his feeble praying. If Jacob had quit praying at a decent bedtime, he would scarcely have survived the next day's meeting with Esau. If the Syrophoenician woman had allowed her faith to faint by silence, humiliation, repulse, or to stop midway in its struggles, her grief-stricken home would never have been brightened by the healing of her daughter.

Pray and never faint is the motto Christ gives us for praying. It is the test of our faith; and the severer the trial and the longer the waiting, the more glorious the results.

The benefits and necessity of importunity are taught by Old Testament saints. Praying men must be strong in hope, and faith, and prayer. They must know how to wait and to press, to wait on God and be in earnest in their approaches to Him.

Abraham has left us an example of importunate intercession in his passionate pleading with God on behalf of Sodom and Gomorrah, and if, as already indicated, he had not ceased in his asking, perhaps God would not have ceased in His giving. "Abraham left off asking before God left off granting." Moses taught the power of importunity when he interceded for Israel forty days and forty nights, by fasting and prayer. And he succeeded in his importunity.

Jesus in His teaching and example illustrated and perfected this principle of Old Testament pleading and waiting. How strange that the only Son of God, who came on a mission direct from His Father, whose only heaven on earth, whose only life and law were to do His Father's will in that mission—what a mystery that He should be under the law of prayer, that the blessings which came to Him were impregnated and purchased by prayer! Stranger still that importunity in prayer was the process by which His wealthiest supplies from God were gained! Had He not prayed with importunity, no transfiguration would have been in His history, no mighty works would have rendered divine His career. His all-night praying was that which filled with compassion and power His all-day work. The importunate praying of His life crowned His death with its triumph. He learned the high lesson of submission to God's will in the struggles of importunate prayer before He illustrated that submission so sublimely on the cross.

"Whether we like it or not," said Mr. Spurgeon, "*asking is the rule of the kingdom.* 'Ask, and ye shall receive.'

wait and to press, to wait on God and be in earnest in
their approaches to Him.

Abraham has left us an example of importunate intercession in his passionate pleading with God on behalf of
Sodom and Gomorrah, and if, as already indicated, he
had not ceased in his asking, perhaps God would not have
ceased in His giving. "Abraham left off asking before
God left off granting." Moses taught the power of importunity when he interceded for Israel forty days and
forty nights, by fasting and prayer. And he succeeded in
his importunity.

Jesus in His teaching and example illustrated and perfected this principle of Old Testament pleading and waiting. How strange that the only Son of God, who came on
a mission direct from His Father, whose only heaven on
earth, whose only life and law were to do His Father's
will in that mission—what a mystery that He should be
under the law of prayer, that the blessings which came to
Him were impregnated and purchased by prayer! Stranger
still that importunity in prayer was the process by which
His wealthiest supplies from God were gained! Had He
not prayed with importunity, no transfiguration would
have been in His history, no mighty works would have
rendered divine His career. His all-night praying was that
which filled with compassion and power His all-day work.
The importunate praying of His life crowned His death
with its triumph. He learned the high lesson of submission to God's will in the struggles of importunate prayer
before He illustrated that submission so sublimely on the
cross.

"Whether we like it or not," said Mr. Spurgeon, "asking is the rule of the kingdom. 'Ask, and ye shall receive.'

the print of a diamond, into our hardest places, and mark with ineffaceable traces our characters. They are the salient periods of our lives, the memorial stones which endure and to which we turn.

Importunity, it may be repeated, is a condition of prayer. We are to press the matter, not with vain repetitions, but with urgent repetitions. We repeat, not to count the times, but to gain the prayer. We cannot quit praying, because heart and soul are in it. We pray "in all perseverance" (Eph 6:18). We hang on to our prayers because by them we live. We press our pleas because we must have them or die. Christ gives us two most expressive parables to emphasize the necessity of importunity in praying. Perhaps Abraham lost Sodom by failing to press to the utmost his privilege of praying. Joash, we know, lost because he stayed his smiting.

Perseverance counts much with God as well as with man. If Elijah had ceased at his first petition, the heavens would have scarcely yielded their rain to his feeble praying. If Jacob had quit praying at a decent bedtime, he would scarcely have survived the next day's meeting with Esau. If the Syrophoenician woman had allowed her faith to faint by silence, humiliation, repulse, or to stop midway in its struggles, her grief-stricken home would never have been brightened by the healing of her daughter.

Pray and never faint is the motto Christ gives us for praying. It is the test of our faith; and the severer the trial and the longer the waiting, the more glorious the results.

The benefits and necessity of importunity are taught by Old Testament saints. Praying men must be strong in hope, and faith, and prayer. They must know how to

on, to wait with unrelaxed and unrelaxable grasp, rest-
less desire, and restful patience. Importunate prayer is
not an incident but the main thing, not a performance
but a passion, not a need but a necessity.

Prayer in its highest form and grandest success assumes
the attitude of a wrestler with God. It is the contest, trial,
and victory of faith; a victory not secured from an enemy,
but from Him who tries our faith that He may enlarge
it, who tests our strength to make us stronger. Few things
give such quickened and permanent vigor to the soul as a
long exhaustive season of importunate prayer. It makes
an experience, an epoch, a new calendar for the spirit, a
new life to religion, a soldierly training. The Bible never
wearies in its pressure and illustration of the fact that the
highest spiritual good is secured as the return of the out-
going of the highest form of spiritual effort. There is
neither encouragement nor room in Bible religion for
feeble desires, listless efforts, lazy attitudes; all must be
strenuous, urgent, ardent. Inflamed desires, impassioned,
unwearied insistence delight heaven. God would have
His children incorrigibly in earnest and persistently bold
in their efforts. Heaven is too busy to listen to halfhearted
prayers.

Our whole being must be in our praying; like John
Knox, we must say and feel, "Give me Scotland, or I die."
Our experience and revelations of God are born of our
costly sacrifice, our costly conflicts, our costly praying.
The wrestling, all-night praying of Jacob made an era
never to be forgotten in Jacob's life, brought God to the
rescue, changed Esau's attitude and conduct, changed
Jacob's character, saved and affected his life, and entered
into the habits of a nation.

Our seasons of importunate prayer cut themselves, like

The case of the Syrophoenician woman is a parable in action. She is arrested in her approaches to Christ by the information that He will not see anyone. She is denied His presence, and then in His presence is treated with seeming indifference, with the chill of silence and unconcern. She presses and approaches, the pressure and approach are repulsed by the stern and crushing statement that He is not sent to her kith or kind, that she is reprobated from His mission and power. She is humiliated by being called a dog. Yet she accepts all, overcomes all, wins all by her humble, dauntless, invincible importunity. The Son of God, pleased, surprised, overpowered by her unconquerable importunity, says to her: "O woman, great is thy faith: be it done unto thee even as thou wilt" (Mt 15:28). Jesus Christ surrenders Himself to the importunity of a great faith. "And shall not God avenge his own elect, that cry to him day and night, and yet he is longsuffering over them?" (Lk 18:7).

Jesus Christ puts the ability to importune as one of the elements of prayer, one of the main conditions of prayer. The prayer of the Syrophoenician woman is an exhibition of the matchless power of importunity, of a conflict more real and involving more of vital energy, endurance, and all the higher elements than was ever illustrated in the conflicts of Isthmia or Olympia.

The first lessons of importunity are taught in the Sermon on the Mount, "Ask, and it shall be given you; seek, and ye shall find; knock, and it shall be opened" (Mt 7:7). These are steps of advance: "For every one that asketh receiveth; and he that seeketh findeth; and to him that knocketh it shall be opened" (v. 8).

Without continuance the prayer may go unanswered. Importunity is made up of the ability to hold on, to press

Time would fail to tell of the mighty things wrought by prayer, for by it holy ones have "subdued kingdoms, wrought righteousness, obtained promises, stopped the mouths of lions, quenched the power of fire, escaped the edge of the sword, from weakness were made strong, waxed mighty in war, turned to flight armies of aliens. Women received their dead by a resurrection" (Heb 11:33-35).

Prayer honors God; it dishonors self. It is man's plea of weakness, ignorance, want, a plea which heaven cannot disregard. God delights to have us pray.

Prayer is not the foe to work; it does not paralyze activity. It works mightily; prayer itself is the greatest work. It springs activity, stimulates desire and effort. Prayer is not an opiate but a tonic; it does not lull to sleep but arouses anew for action. The lazy man does not, will not, cannot pray, for prayer demands energy. Paul calls it a striving, an agony. With Jacob it was a wrestling; with the Syrophoenician woman it was a struggle which called into play all the higher qualities of the soul, and which demanded great force to meet.

The closet is not an asylum for the indolent and worthless Christian. It is not a nursery where none but babes belong. It is the battlefield of the Church, its citadel, the scene of heroic and unearthly conflicts. The closet is the base of supplies for the Christian and the Church. Cut off from it there is nothing left but retreat and disaster. The energy for work, the mastery over self, the deliverance from fear, all spiritual results and graces, are much advanced by prayer. The difference between the strength, the experience, the holiness of Christians is found in the contrast in their praying.

Few, short, and feeble prayers betoken a low spiritual

condition. Men ought to pray much and to apply themselves to it with energy and perseverance. Eminent Christians have been eminent in prayer. The deep things of
God are learned nowhere else. Great things for God are
done by great prayers. He who prays much, studies much,
loves much, and works much does much for God and
humanity. The execution of the Gospel, the vigor of
faith, the maturity and excellence of spiritual graces wait
on prayer.

*"Nothing is impossible to industry," said one of the
seven sages of Greece. Let us change the word industry
for persevering prayer, and the motto will be more
Christian and more worthy of universal adoption. I am
persuaded that we are all more deficient in a spirit of
prayer than in any other grace. God loves importunate
prayer so much that He will not give us much blessing
without it. And the reason that He loves such prayer is
that He loves us and knows that it is a necessary preparation for our receiving the richest blessings which He is
waiting and longing to bestow.*

6

IMPORTUNITY: CHARACTERISTIC OF REAL PRAYER

CHRIST PUTS IMPORTUNITY as a distinguishing characteristic of true praying. We must not only pray, but we must pray with great urgency, with intentness, and with repetition. We must not only pray, but we must pray again and again. We must not get tired of praying. We must be thoroughly in earnest, deeply concerned about the things for which we ask, for Jesus Christ made it very plain that the secret of prayer and its success lie in its urgency. We must press our prayers upon God.

In a parable of exquisite pathos and simplicity, our Lord taught not simply that men ought to pray, but that men ought to pray with full heartiness, and press the matter with vigorous energy and brave hearts.

"And he spake a parable unto them to the end that they ought always to pray, and not to faint; saying, There was in a city a judge, which feared not God, and regarded not man: and there was a widow in that city; and she came oft unto him, saying, Avenge me of mine adversary. And he would not for a while: but afterward he said within himself, Though I fear not God, nor regard man; yet because this widow troubleth me, I will avenge her, lest she wear me out by her continual coming. And the Lord said, Hear what the unrighteous judge saith. And

45

shall not God avenge his elect, which cry to him day and night, and he is long-suffering over them? I say unto you, that he will avenge them speedily. Nevertheless, when the Son of man cometh, shall he find faith on the earth?" (Lk 18:1-8).

This poor woman's case was a most hopeless one, but importunity brings hope from the realms of despair and creates success where neither success nor its conditions existed. There could be no stronger case to show how unwearied and dauntless importunity gains its ends where everything else fails. The preface to this parable says: "He spake a parable . . . to the end that they ought always to pray, and not to faint." He knew that men would soon get fainthearted in praying, so to hearten us He gives this picture of the marvelous power of importunity.

The widow, weak and helpless, is helplessness personified; bereft of every hope and influence which could move an unjust judge, she yet wins her case solely by her tireless and aggressive importunity. Could the necessity of importunity, its power and tremendous importance in prayer, be pictured in deeper or more impressive coloring? It surmounts or removes all obstacles, overcomes every resisting force, and gains its ends in the face of invincible hindrances. We can do nothing without prayer. All things can be done by importunate prayer.

That is the teaching of Jesus Christ.

Another parable spoken by Jesus enforces the same great truth. A man at midnight goes to his friend for a loan of bread. His pleas are strong, based on friendship and the embarrassing and exacting demands of necessity, but these all fail. He gets no bread, but he stays and presses, and waits and gains. Sheer importunity succeeds where all other pleas and influences had failed.

It is a rule that never will be altered in anybody's case. Our Lord Jesus Christ is the elder brother of the family, but God has not relaxed the rule for Him. Remember this text: Jehovah says to His own Son, 'Ask of me, and I will give thee the heathen for thine inheritance, and the uttermost parts of the earth for thy possession.' If the royal and divine Son of God cannot be exempted from the rule of asking that He may have, you and I cannot expect the rule to be relaxed in our favor. Why should it be? What reason can be pleaded why we should be exempted from prayer? What argument can there be why we should be deprived of the privilege and delivered from the necessity of supplication? I can see none, can you? God will bless Elijah and send rain on Israel, but Elijah must pray for it. If the chosen nation is to prosper, Samuel must plead for it. If the Jews are to be delivered, Daniel must intercede. God will bless Paul, and the nations shall be converted through him, but Paul must pray. Pray he did without ceasing; his epistles show that he expected nothing except by asking for it. If you may have everything by asking, and nothing without asking, I beg you to see how absolutely vital prayer is, and I beseech you to abound in it."

There is not the least doubt that much of our praying fails for lack of persistency. It is without the fire and strength of perseverance. Persistence is of the essence of true praying. It may not be always called into exercise, but it must be there as the reserve force. Jesus taught that perseverance is the essential element of prayer. Men must be in earnest when they kneel at God's footstool.

Too often we get fainthearted and quit praying at the point where we ought to begin. We let go at the very

point where we should hold on strongest. Our prayers
are weak because they are not impassioned by an unfailing and resistless will.

God loves the importunate pleader, and sends him answers that would never have been granted but for the
persistency that refuses to let go until the petition craved
for is granted.

*It is good, I find, to persevere in attempts to pray. If I
cannot pray with perseverance or continue long in my
addresses to the Divine Being, I have found that the more
I do in secret prayer the more I have delight to do, and
have enjoyed more of the spirit of prayer; and frequently
I have found the contrary, when by journeying or otherwise, I have been deprived of retirement.*

DAVID BRAINERD

7

INTIMACY WITH GOD

THEY OUGHT ALWAYS TO PRAY, and not to faint" (Lk 18:1). The words are the words of our Lord, who not only ever sought to impress upon His followers the urgency and the importance of prayer, but set them an example which they, alas, have been far too slow to copy.

The *always* speaks for itself. Prayer is not a meaningless function or duty to be crowded into the busy or the weary ends of the day, and we are not obeying our Lord's command when we content ourselves with a few minutes upon our knees in the morning rush or late at night when the faculties, tired with the tasks of the day, call out for rest. God is always within call, it is true; His ear is ever attentive to the cry of His child, but we can never get to know Him if we use the vehicle of prayer as we use the telephone, for a few words of hurried conversation. Intimacy requires development. We can never know God as it is our privilege to know Him, by brief and fragmentary and unconsidered repetitions of intercessions that are requests for personal favors and nothing more. That is not the way in which we can come into communication with heaven's King. "The goal of prayer is the ear of God," a goal that can only be reached by patient and continued and continuous waiting upon Him, pouring out our heart to Him and permitting Him to speak to us. Only by so doing can we expect to know Him, and as we come to know Him better we shall spend more time in His presence and find that presence a constant and ever increasing delight.

Always does not mean that we are to neglect the ordinary duties of life. What it means is that the soul which has come into intimate contact with God in the silence of the prayer chamber is never out of conscious touch with the Father, that the heart is always going out to Him in loving communion, and that the moment the mind is released from the task upon which it is engaged it returns as naturally to God as the bird does to its nest. What a beautiful conception of prayer we get if we regard it in this light, if we view it as a constant fellowship, an unbroken audience with the King! Prayer then loses every vestige of dread which it may once have possessed; we regard it no longer as a duty which must be performed, but rather as a privilege which is to be enjoyed, a rare delight that is always revealing some new beauty.

Thus, when we open our eyes in the morning, our thought instantly mounts heavenward. To many Christians the morning hours are the most precious portion of the day, because they provide the opportunity for the hallowed fellowship that gives the keynote to the day's program. And what better introduction can there be to the never ceasing glory and wonder of a new day than to spend it alone with God? It is said that Mr. Moody, at a time when no other place was available, kept his morning watch in the coal shed, pouring out his heart to God, and finding in his precious Bible a true "feast of fat things."

George Mueller also combined Bible study with prayer in the quiet morning hours. At one time his practice was to give himself to prayer after having dressed in the morning. Then his plan underwent a change. As he himself put it: "I saw the most important thing I had to do was to give myself to the reading of the Word of God, and to meditation on it, that thus my heart might be comforted, encouraged, warned, reproved, instructed; and that thus, by means of the Word of God, whilst meditating on it, my heart might be brought into experimental communion with the Lord. I began, therefore, to meditate on the New Testament early in the morning. The first thing I did, after having asked in a few words for the Lord's blessing upon His precious Word, was to begin to meditate on the Word of God, searching, as it were, into every verse to get blessing out of it; not for the sake of the public ministry of the Word, not for the sake of preaching on what I had meditated on, but for the sake of obtaining food for my own soul. The result I have found to be almost invariably thus, that after a very few minutes my soul has been led to confession, or to thanksgiving, or to intercession, or to supplication; so that, though I did not, as it were, give myself to prayer, but to meditation, yet it turned almost immediately more or less into prayer."

The study of the Word and prayer go together, and where we find the one truly practiced, the other is sure to be seen in close alliance.

But we do not pray always. That is the trouble with so many of us. We need to pray much more than we do, and much longer than we do.

Robert Murray McCheyne, gifted and saintly, of whom it was said, that "Whether viewed as a son, a brother, a friend, or a pastor, he was the most faultless and attractive exhibition of the true Christian they had ever seen embodied in a living form," knew what it was to spend much time upon his knees, and he never wearied in urging upon others the joy and the value of holy intercession. "God's children should pray," he said. "They should cry day and night unto Him. God hears every one of your cries in the busy hour of the daytime and in the lonely watches of the night." In every way, by preaching, by exhortation when present, and by letters when absent, McCheyne emphasized the vital duty of prayer, importunate and unceasing prayer.

In his diary we find this: "In the morning was engaged in preparing the head, then the heart. This has been frequently my error, and I have always felt the evil of it, especially in prayer. Reform it then, O Lord." While on his trip to the Holy Land he wrote: "For much of our safety I feel indebted to the prayers of my people. If the veil of the world's machinery were lifted off how much we would find done in answer to the prayers of God's children!" In an ordination sermon he said to the preacher: "Give yourself to prayers and the ministry of the Word. If you do not pray, God will probably lay you aside from your ministry, as He did me, to teach you to pray. Remember Luther's maxim, 'To have prayed well is to have studied well.' Get your texts, your thoughts, your words, from God. Carry the names of the little flock upon your breast like the High Priest. Wrestle for the unconverted. Luther spent his best three hours in prayer; John Welch prayed seven or eight hours a day. He used to keep a plaid on his bed that he might wrap himself in when he rose during the night. Sometimes his wife found him on the ground lying weeping. When she complained, he would say, 'O woman, I have the souls of three thousand to answer for, and I know not how it is with many of them.' " The people he exhorted and charged: "Pray for your pastor. Pray for his body, that he may be kept

strong and spared many years. Pray for his soul, that he
may be kept humble and holy, a burning and shining
light. Pray for his ministry, that it may be abundantly
blessed, that he may be anointed to preach good tidings.
Let there be no secret prayer without naming him before
your God, no family prayer without carrying your pastor
in your hearts to God."

"Two things," says his biographer, "he seems never to
have ceased from—the cultivation of personal holiness and
the most anxious efforts to win souls." The two are the
inseparable attendants on the ministry of prayer. Prayer
fails when the desire and effort for personal holiness fail.
No person is a soul-winner who is not adept in the ministry of prayer. "It is the duty of ministers," says this
holy man, "to begin the reformation of religion and manner with themselves, families, etc., with confession of past
sin, earnest prayer for direction, grace and full purpose of
heart." He begins with himself under the head of "Reformation in Secret Prayer," and he resolves:

"I ought not omit any of the parts of prayer—confession, adoration, thanksgiving, petition and intercession.
There is a fearful tendency to omit *confession* proceeding
from low views of God and His law, slight views of my
heart, and the sin of my past life. This must be resisted.
There is a constant tendency to omit *adoration* when I
forget to whom I am speaking, when I rush heedlessly into
the presence of Jehovah without thought of His awful
name and charcter. When I have little eyesight for His
glory, and little admiration of His wonders, I have the
native tendency of the heart to omit giving *thanks,* and
yet it is specially commanded.

"Often when the heart is dead to the salvation of others
I omit *intercession,* and yet it especially is the spirit of

the great Advocate who has the name of Israel on His heart, I ought to pray before seeing anyone. Often when I sleep long, or meet with others early, and then have family prayer and breakfast and forenoon callers, it is eleven or twelve o'clock before I begin secret prayer. This is a wretched system; it is unscriptural. Christ rose before day and went into a solitary place. David says, 'Early will I seek thee; thou shalt early hear my voice.' Mary Magdalene came to the sepulchre while it was yet dark. Family prayer loses much of its power and sweetness; and I can do no good to those who come to seek from me. The conscience feels guilty, the soul unfed, the lamp not trimmed. I feel it is far better to begin with God, to see His face first, to get my soul near Him before it is near another. 'When I awake I am still with thee.' If I have slept too long, or I am going an early journey, or my time is in any way shortened, it is best to dress hurriedly and have a few minutes alone with God than to give up all for lost. But in general it is best to have at least one hour alone with God before engaging in anything else. I ought to spend the best hours of the day in communion with God. When I awake in the night, I ought to rise and pray as David and John Welch."

McCheyne believed in being *always* in prayer, and his fruitful life, short though that life was, affords an illustration of the power that comes from long and frequent visits to the secret place where we keep tryst with our Lord.

Men of McCheyne's stamp are needed today—praying men who know how to give themselves to the greatest task demanding their time and their attention, men who can give their whole heart to the holy task of intercession, men who can pray through. God's cause is committed to

more reading, retirement and private devotion, I have
little mastery over my own tempers. An unhappy day to
me for want of more solitude and prayer. If there be any-
thing I do, if there be anything I leave undone, let me be
perfect in prayer.

After all, whatever God may appoint, prayer is the great
thing. Oh, that I may be a man of prayer!

HENRY MARTYN

men; God commits Himself to men. Praying men are the
vicegerents of God; they do His work and carry out His
plans.

We are obliged to pray if we are citizens of God's Kingdom. Prayerlessness is expatriation, or worse, from God's
Kingdom. It is outlawry, a high crime, a constitutional
breach. The Christian who relegates prayer to a subor-
dinate place in his life soon loses whatever spiritual zeal
he may have once possessed, and the church that makes
little of prayer cannot maintain vital piety and is power-
less to advance the Gospel. The Gospel cannot live, fight,
or conquer without prayer—prayer unceasing, instant, and
ardent.

Little prayer is the characteristic of a backslidden age
and of a backslidden church. Whenever there is little
praying in the pulpit or in the pew, spiritual bankruptcy
is imminent and inevitable.

The cause of God has no commercial age, no cultured
age, no age of education, no age of money. But it has one
golden age, and that is the age of prayer. When its leaders are men of prayer, when prayer is the prevailing element of worship, like the incense giving continual fragrance to its service, then the cause of God will be tri-
umphant.

Better praying and more of it, that is what we need.
We need holier men, and more of them, holier women,
and more of them to pray—women like Hannah, who, out
of their greatest griefs and temptations brewed their greatest prayers. Through prayer Hannah found her relief.
Everywhere the believers were backslidden and apostate;
their foes were victorious. Hannah gave herself to prayer,
and in sorrow she multiplied her praying. She saw a great
revival born of her praying. When the whole nation

was oppressed, Samuel, prophet and priest, was born to establish a new line of priesthood, and her praying warmed into life a new life for God. Everywhere religion revived and flourished. God, true to His promise, *Ask of Me*, though the praying came from a woman's broken heart, heard and answered, sending a new day of holy gladness to revive His people.

So once more, let us apply the emphasis and repeat that the great need of the Church in this and all ages is men of such commanding faith, of such unsullied holiness, of such marked spiritual vigor and consuming zeal that they will work spiritual revolutions through their mighty praying. "Natural ability and educational advantages do not figure as factors in this matter; but a capacity for faith, the ability to pray, the power of a thorough consecration, the ability of self-littleness, an absolute losing of one's self in God's glory and an ever present and insatiable yearning and seeking after all the fullness of God. Men who can set the Church ablaze for God, not in a noisy, showy way, but with an intense and quiet heat that melts and moves everything for God."

And, to return to the vital point, secret praying is the test, the gauge, the conserver of man's relation to God. The prayer chamber, while it is the test of the sincerity of our devotion to God, becomes also the measure of the devotion. The self-denial, the sacrifices which we make for our prayer chambers, the frequency of our visits to that hallowed place of meeting with the Lord, the lingering to stay, the loathness to leave, are values which we put on communion alone with God, the price we pay for the Spirit's trysting hours of heavenly love.

The prayer chamber conserves our relation to God. It hems every raw edge; it tucks up every flowing and en-

tangling garment, girds up every fainting loin. The sheet anchor holds not the ship more surely and safely than the prayer chamber holds to God. Satan has to break our hold on, and close up our way to, the prayer chambers, ere he can break our hold on God or close up our way to heaven.

> Be not afraid to pray; to pray is right;
>   Pray if thou canst with hope, but ever pray,
> Though hope be weak or sick with long delay;
>   Pray in the darkness if there be no light;
> And if for any wish thou dare not pray
>   Then pray to God to cast that wish away.

In God's name I beseech you let prayer nourish yo soul as your meals nourish your body. Let your fixed sons of prayer keep you in God's presence through day, and His presence frequently remembered thro be an ever-fresh spring of prayer. Such a brief, lov ollection of God renews a man's whole being, q passions, supplies light and counsel in difficulty, subdues the temper, and causes him to possess patience, or rather gives it up to the possessio

Devoted too much time and attention public duties of the ministry. But this h duct, for I have learned that neglect of communion with God in meditation (way to redeem the time nor to fit trations.

I rightly attribute my present d cient time and tranquility for p

8

PRAYER, THE REMEDY FOR ALL EVILS

THAT THE MEN had quit praying in Paul's time we cannot certainly affirm. They have, in the main, quit praying now. They are too busy to pray. Time and strength and every faculty are laid under tribute to money, to business, to the affairs of the world. Few men lay themselves out in great praying. The great business of praying is a hurried, petty, starved, beggarly business with most men.

Paul calls a halt, and lays a levy on men for prayer. Put the men to praying is Paul's unfailing remedy for great evils in church, in state, in politics, in business, and in the home. Put the men to praying, then politics will be cleansed, business will be thriftier, the Church will be holier, the home will be sweeter.

"I exhort, therefore, *first of all,* that supplications, prayers, intercessions, thanksgivings, be made for all men; for kings and all that are in high place; that we may lead a tranquil and quiet life in all godliness and gravity. This is good and acceptable in the sight of God our Saviour. I desire therefore that the men pray in every place, lifting up holy hands, without wrath and disputing" (1 Ti 2:1-3, 8, italics added).

Praying women and children are invaluable to God, but if their praying is not supplemented by praying men, there will be a great loss in the power of prayer, a great breach and depreciation in the value of prayer, great paralysis in the energy of the Gospel. Jesus Christ spoke a parable unto the people, telling them that men ought always to pray and not faint. Men who are strong in everything else ought to be strong in prayer, and never yield to discouragement, weakness, or depression. Men who are brave, persistent, and redoubtable in other pursuits ought to be full of courage, unfainting, and strong-hearted in prayer.

Men are to pray; all men are to pray. Men, as distinguished from women; men in their strength, in their wisdom. There is an absolute, specific command that the men pray; there is an absolute, imperative necessity that men pray. The first of beings, man, should also be first in prayer.

In the admonition in verse 8, Paul deals with the men in contrast to, and distinct from, the women. The men are definitely commanded, seriously charged, and warmly exhorted to pray. Perhaps it was that men were averse to prayer, or indifferent to it; it may be that they deemed it a small thing, and gave to it neither time nor value nor significance. But God would have all men pray, and so the great apostle lifts the subject into prominence and emphasizes its importance.

For prayer is of transcendent importance. Prayer is the mightiest agent to advance God's work. Only praying hearts and hands can do God's work. Prayer succeeds when all else fails. Prayer has won great victories and rescued, with notable triumph, God's saints when every other hope was gone. Men who know how to pray are the greatest boon God can give to earth; they are the richest gift earth can offer heaven. Men who know how to use this weapon of prayer are God's best soldiers, His mightiest leaders.

Praying men are God's chosen leaders. The distinction between the leaders that God brings to the front to lead and bless His people, and those leaders who owe their position of leadership to a worldly, selfish, unsanctified selection, is this: God's leaders are preeminently men of prayer. This distinguishes them as the simple, divine attestation of their call, the seal of their separation by God. Whatever of other graces or gifts they may have, the gift and grace of prayer towers above them all. In whatever else they may share or differ, in the gift of prayer they are one.

What would God's leaders be without prayer? Strip Moses of his power in prayer, a gift that made him eminent in pagan estimate, and the crown is taken from his head, the food and fire of his faith are gone. Elijah without his praying would have neither record nor place in the divine legation; his life insipid, cowardly; its energy, defiance, and fire gone. Without Elijah's praying the Jordan would never have yielded to the stroke of his mantle, nor would the stern angel of death have honored him with the chariot and horses of fire. The argument that God used to quiet the fears and convince Ananias of Paul's condition and sincerity is the epitome of his history, the solution of his life and work: "Behold he prayeth."

Paul, Luther, Wesley—what would these chosen ones of God be without the distinguishing and controlling element of prayer? They were leaders for God because they were mighty in prayer. They were not leaders because of brilliancy in thought, because of being exhaustless in resources, because of their magnificent culture or native endowment, but they were leaders because by the power of prayer they could command the power of God. Praying men mean much more than men who say prayers, much more than men who pray by habit. It means men with whom prayer is a mighty force, an energy that moves heaven and pours untold treasures of good on earth.

Praying men are the safety of the Church from the materialism that is affecting all its plans and polity, and which is hardening its lifeblood. The insinuation circulates as a secret, deadly poison that the Church is not so dependent on purely spiritual forces as it used to be, that changed times and changed conditions have brought it out of its spiritual straits and dependencies and put it where other forces can bear it to its climax. A fatal snare of this kind has allured the Church into worldly embraces, dazzled her leaders, weakened her foundations, and shorn her of much of her beauty and strength. Praying men are the saviors of the Church from this material tendency. They pour into it the original spiritual forces, lift it off the sandbars of materialism, and press it out into the ocean depths of spiritual power. Praying men keep God in the Church in full force, keep His hand on the helm, and train the Church in its lessons of strength and trust.

The number and efficiency of the laborers in God's vineyard in all lands is dependent on the men of prayer. The mightiness of these men of prayer increases, by the divinely arranged process, the number and success of the consecrated labors. Prayer opens wide their doors of access, gives holy aptness to enter, and holy boldness, firmness, and fruitage. Praying men are needed in all fields of spiritual labor. There is no position in the Church of God, high or low, which can be well-filled without instant prayer. There is no position where Christians are found that does not demand the full play of a faith that always prays and never faints. Praying men are needed in the house of God that they may order and direct trade, not

men; God commits Himself to men. Praying men are the
vicegerents of God; they do His work and carry out His
plans.

We are obliged to pray if we are citizens of God's Kingdom. Prayerlessness is expatriation, or worse, from God's
Kingdom. It is outlawry, a high crime, a constitutional
breach. The Christian who relegates prayer to a subor-
dinate place in his life soon loses whatever spiritual zeal
he may have once possessed, and the church that makes
little of prayer cannot maintain vital piety and is power-
less to advance the Gospel. The Gospel cannot live, fight,
or conquer without prayer—prayer unceasing, instant, and
ardent.

Little prayer is the characteristic of a backslidden age
and of a backslidden church. Whenever there is little
praying in the pulpit or in the pew, spiritual bankruptcy
is imminent and inevitable.

The cause of God has no commercial age, no cultured
age, no age of education, no age of money. But it has one
golden age, and that is the age of prayer. When its leaders are men of prayer, when prayer is the prevailing element of worship, like the incense giving continual fragrance to its service, then the cause of God will be tri-
umphant.

Better praying and more of it, that is what we need.
We need holier men, and more of them, holier women,
and more of them to pray—women like Hannah, who, out
of their greatest griefs and temptations brewed their greatest prayers. Through prayer Hannah found her relief.
Everywhere the believers were backslidden and apostate;
their foes were victorious. Hannah gave herself to prayer,
and in sorrow she multiplied her praying. She saw a great
revival born of her praying. When the whole nation

was oppressed, Samuel, prophet and priest, was born to establish a new line of priesthood, and her praying warmed into life a new life for God. Everywhere religion revived and flourished. God, true to His promise, *Ask of Me,* though the praying came from a woman's broken heart, heard and answered, sending a new day of holy gladness to revive His people.

So once more, let us apply the emphasis and repeat that the great need of the Church in this and all ages is men of such commanding faith, of such unsullied holiness, of such marked spiritual vigor and consuming zeal that they will work spiritual revolutions through their mighty praying. "Natural ability and educational advantages do not figure as factors in this matter; but a capacity for faith, the ability to pray, the power of a thorough consecration, the ability of self-littleness, an absolute losing of one's self in God's glory and an ever present and insatiable yearning and seeking after all the fullness of God. Men who can set the Church ablaze for God, not in a noisy, showy way, but with an intense and quiet heat that melts and moves everything for God."

And, to return to the vital point, secret praying is the test, the gauge, the conserver of man's relation to God. The prayer chamber, while it is the test of the sincerity of our devotion to God, becomes also the measure of the devotion. The self-denial, the sacrifices which we make for our prayer chambers, the frequency of our visits to that hallowed place of meeting with the Lord, the lingering to stay, the loathness to leave, are values which we put on communion alone with God, the price we pay for the Spirit's trysting hours of heavenly love.

The prayer chamber conserves our relation to God. It hems every raw edge; it tucks up every flowing and entangling garment, girds up every fainting loin. The sheet anchor holds not the ship more surely and safely than the prayer chamber holds to God. Satan has to break our hold on, and close up our way to, the prayer chambers, ere he can break our hold on God or close up our way to heaven.

> Be not afraid to pray; to pray is right;
>   Pray if thou canst with hope, but ever pray,
> Though hope be weak or sick with long delay;
>   Pray in the darkness if there be no light;
> And if for any wish thou dare not pray
>   Then pray to God to cast that wish away.

In God's name I beseech you let prayer nourish your soul as your meals nourish your body. Let your fixed seasons of prayer keep you in God's presence through the day, and His presence frequently remembered through it be an ever-fresh spring of prayer. Such a brief, loving recollection of God renews a man's whole being, quiets his passions, supplies light and counsel in difficulty, gradually subdues the temper, and causes him to possess his soul in patience, or rather gives it up to the possession of God.

FENELON

Devoted too much time and attention to outward and public duties of the ministry. But this has a mistaken conduct, for I have learned that neglect of much and fervent communion with God in meditation and prayer is not the way to redeem the time nor to fit me for public ministrations.

I rightly attribute my present deadness to want of sufficient time and tranquility for private devotion. Want of more reading, retirement and private devotion, I have little mastery over my own tempers. An unhappy day to me for want of more solitude and prayer. If there be anything I do, if there be anything I leave undone, let me be perfect in prayer.

After all, whatever God may appoint, prayer is the great thing. Oh, that I may be a man of prayer!

HENRY MARTYN

according to the maxims of this world, but according to Bible precepts and the maxims of the heavenly life.

Men of prayer are needed especially in the positions of church influence, honor, and power. These leaders of church thought, of church work, and of church life should be men of signal power in prayer. It is the praying heart that sanctifies the toil and skill of the hands, and the toil and wisdom of the head. Prayer keeps work in the line of God's will, and keeps thought in the line of God's Word. The solemn responsibilities of leadership, in a large or limited sphere in God's Church, should be so hedged about with prayer that between it and the world there should be an impassable gulf, so elevated and purified by prayer that neither cloud nor night should stain the radiance or dim the sight of a constant meridian view of God. Many church leaders seem to think if they can be prominent as men of business, of money, of influence, of thought, of plans, of scholarly attainments, of eloquent gifts, of conspicuous activities, that these are enough and will atone for the absence of the higher spiritual power which only much praying can give. But how vain and paltry are these in the serious work of bringing glory to God, controlling the Church for Him, and bringing it into full accord with its divine mission!

Praying men are men that have done so much for God in the past. They are the ones who have won the victories for God and spoiled His foes. They are the ones who have set up His Kingdom in the very camps of His enemies. There are no other conditions of success in this day. The twentieth century has no relief statute to suspend the necessity or force of prayer, no substitute by which its gracious ends can be secured. We are shut up to this: praying hands only can build for God. They are God's mighty ones on earth, His master builders. They may be destitute of all else, but with the wrestlings and prevailings of a simple-hearted faith they are mighty, the mightiest for God. Church leaders may be gifted in all else, but without this greatest of gifts they are as Samson shorn of his locks, or as the Temple without the divine presence or the divine glory, and on whose altars the heavenly flame has died.

The only protection and rescue from worldliness lie in our intense and radical spirituality; and our only hope for the existence and maintenance of this high, saving spirituality, under God, is in the purest and most aggressive leadership, a leadership that knows the secret power of prayer, the sign by which the Church has conquered, and that has conscience, conviction, and courage to hold her true to her symbols, true to her traditions, and true to the hidings of her power. We need this prayerful leadership; we must have it, that by the perfection and beauty of its holiness, by the strength and elevation of its faith, by the potency and pressure of its prayers, by the authority and spotlessness of its example, by the fire and contagion of its zeal, by the singularity, sublimity, and unworldliness of its piety, it may influence God and hold and mold the Church to its heavenly pattern.

How mightily such leaders are felt! How their flame arouses the Church! How they stir it by the force of their Pentecostal presence! How they embattle and give victory by the conflicts and triumphs of their own faith! How they fashion it by the impress and importunity of their prayers! How they inoculate it by the contagion and fire of their holiness! How they lead the march in great spiritual revolutions! How the Church is raised from the dead by the resurrection call of their sermons! Holiness springs up in their wake as flowers at the voice of spring, and where they tread the desert blooms as the garden of the Lord. God's cause demands such leaders along the whole line of official position from subaltern to superior. How feeble, aimless, or worldly are our efforts, how demoralized and vain for God's work without them!

The gift of these leaders is not in the range of ecclesiastical power. They are God's gifts. Their being, their presence, their number, and their ability are the tokens of His favor; their lack is the sure sign of His disfavor, the presage of His withdrawal. Let the Church of God be on her knees before the Lord of hosts, that He may more mightily endow the leaders we already have, and put others in rank, and lead all along the line of our embattled front.

The world is coming into the Church at many points and many ways. It oozes in, it pours in, it comes in with brazen front or soft, insinuating disguise, it comes in at the top and comes in at the bottom, and percolates through many a hidden way.

For praying men and holy men we are looking, for men whose presence in the Church will make it like a censer of holiest incense flaming up to God. With God the man counts for everything. Rites, forms, organizations are of small moment; unless they are backed by the holiness of the man, they are offensive in His sight. "Incense is an abomination unto me; new moons and sabbath, the calling of assemblies—I cannot away with iniquity and the solemn meeting" (Is 1:13).

Why does God speak so strongly against His own ordinances? Personal purity had failed. The impure man tainted all the sacred institutions of God and defiled them. God regards the man in so important a way as to put a

kind of discount on all else. Men have built Him glorious
temples and have striven and exhausted themselves to
please God by all manner of gifts, but in lofty strains He
has rebuked these proud worshipers and rejected their
princely gifts.

"Heaven is my throne, and the earth is my footstool:
What manner of house will ye build unto me? And what
place shall be my rest? For all these things hath my hand
made, and so all these things came to be, saith Jehovah....
He that killeth an ox is as he that slayeth a man; he that
sacrificeth a lamb, as he that breaketh a dog's neck; he
that offereth an oblation, as he that offereth swine's blood;
he that burneth frankincense, as he that blesseth an idol."
Turning away in disgust from these costly and profane
offerings, He declares, "But to this man will I look, even
to him that is poor and of a contrite spirit, and trembleth
at my word" (Is 66:1-3) .

This truth that God regards the personal purity of the
man is fundamental. This truth suffers when ordinances
are made much of and forms of worship multiply. The
man and his spiritual character depreciate as church cere-
monials increase. The simplicity of worship is lost in religious aesthetics or in the gaudiness of religious forms.

This truth that the personal purity of the individual is
the only thing God cares for is lost sight of when the
church begins to estimate men for what they have. When
the church eyes a man's money, social standing, his be-
longings in any way, then spiritual values are at a fearful
discount, and the tear of penitence and the heaviness of
guilt are never seen at her portals. Worldly bribes have
opened and stained its pearly gates by the entrance of the
impure.

This truth that God is looking after personal purity is

swallowed up when the church has a greed for numbers. "Not numbers, but personal purity is our aim," said the fathers of Methodism. The parading of church statistics is mightily against the grain of spiritual religion. Eyeing numbers greatly hinders the looking after personal purity. The increase of quantity is generally at a loss of quality. Bulk abates preciousness.

The age of church organization and church machinery is not an age noted for elevated and strong personal piety. Machinery looks for engineers and organizations for generals, and not for saints, to run them. The simplest organization may aid purity as well as strength; but beyond that narrow limit, organization swallows up the individual and is careless of personal purity; push, activity, enthusiasm, and zeal for an organization come in as the vicious substitutes for spiritual character. Holiness and all the spiritual graces of hardy culture and slow growth are discarded as too slow and too costly for the progress and rush of the age. By dint of machinery, new organizations, and spiritual weakness, results are vainly expected to be secured which can only be secured by faith, prayer, and waiting on God.

The man and his spiritual character is what God is looking after. If men, holy men, can be turned out by the easy processes of church machinery readier and better than by the old-time processes, we would gladly invest in every new and improved patent; but we do not believe it. We adhere to the old way, the way the holy prophets went, the king's highway of holiness.

An example of this is afforded by the case of William Wilberforce. High in social position, a member of Parliament, the friend of Pitt, the famous statesman, he was not called of God to forsake his high social position nor to

quit Parliament, but he was called to order his life according to the pattern set by Jesus Christ and to give himself
to prayer. To read the story of his life is to be impressed
with its holiness and its devotion to the claims of the
quiet hours alone with God. His conversion was an-
nounced to his friends—to Pitt and others—by letter.

In the beginning of his religious career he recorded:
"My chief reasons for a day of secret prayer are (1) That
the state of public affairs is very critical and calls for
earnest deprecation of the Divine displeasure. (2) My
station in life is a very difficult one, wherein I am at a loss
to know how to act. Direction, therefore, should be specially sought from time to time. (3) I have been gracious-
ly supported in difficult situations of a public nature. I
have gone out and returned home in safety, and found a
kind reception has attended me. I would humbly hope,
too, that what I am now doing is a proof that God has not
withdrawn His Holy Spirit from me. I am covered with
mercies."

The recurrence of his birthday led him again to review his situation and employment. "I find," he wrote,
"that books alienate my heart from God as much as anything. I have been framing a plan of study for myself,
but let me remember but one thing is needful, that if my
heart cannot be kept in a spiritual state without so much
prayer, meditation, Scripture reading, etc., as are incom-
patible with study, I must *seek first* the righteousness of
God." All were to be surrendered for spiritual advance.
"I fear," we find him saying, "that I have not studied the
Scriptures enough. Surely in the summer recess I ought
to read the Scriptures an hour or two every day, besides
prayer, devotional reading and meditation. God will
prosper me better if I wait on Him. The experience of all

good men shows that without constant prayer and watchfulness the life of God in the soul stagnates. Doddridge's morning and evening devotions were serious matters. Colonel Gardiner always spent hours in prayer in the morning before he went forth. Bonnell practiced private devotions largely morning and evening, and repeated Psalms dressing and undressing to raise his mind to heavenly things. I would look up to God to make the means effectual. I fear that my devotions are too much hurried, that I do not read Scripture enough. I must grow in grace; I must love God more; I must feel the power of Divine things more. Whether I am more or less learned signifies not. Whether even I execute the work which I deem useful is comparatively unimportant. But beware, my soul, of luke-warmness."

The New Year began with the Holy Communion and new vows. "I will press forward," he wrote, "and labor to know God better and love Him more. Assuredly I may, because God will give His Holy Spirit to them that ask Him, and the Holy Spirit will shed abroad the love of God in the heart. Oh, then, pray, pray; be earnest, press forward and follow on to know the Lord. Without watchfulness, humiliation and prayer, the sense of Divine things must languish." To prepare for the future, he said he found nothing more effectual than private prayer and the serious perusal of the New Testament.

And again: "I must put down that I have lately too little time for private devotions. I can sadly confirm Doddridge's remark that when we go on ill in the closet we commonly do so everywhere else. I must mend here. I am afraid of getting into what Owen calls the trade of sinning and repenting . . . Lord help me, the shortening of private devotions starves the soul; it grows lean and faint. This must not be. I must redeem more time. I see how lean in spirit I become without full allowance of time for private devotions; I must be careful to be watching unto prayer."

At another time he puts on record: "I must try what I long ago heard was the rule of E———, the great upholsterer, who, when he came from Bond Street to his little villa, always first retired to his closet. I have been keeping too late hours, and hence have had but a hurried half hour to myself. Surely the experience of all good men confirms the proposition, that without due measure of private devotions, the soul will grow lean."

To his son he wrote: "Let me conjure you not to be seduced into neglecting, curtailing or hurrying over your morning prayers. Of all things, guard against neglecting God in the closet. There is nothing more fatal to the life and power of religion. More solitude and earlier hours—prayer three times a day at least. How much better might I serve if I cultivated a closer communion with God!"

Wilberforce knew the secret of a holy life. Is that not where most of us fail? We are so busy with other things, so immersed even in doing good and in carrying on the Lord's work, that we neglect the quiet seasons of prayer with God; and before we are aware of it, our soul is lean and impoverished.

"One night alone in prayer," says Spurgeon, "might make us new men, changed from poverty of soul to spiritual wealth, from trembling to triumphing. We have an example of it in the life of Jacob. Aforetime the crafty shuffler, always bargaining and calculating, unlovely in almost every respect, yet one night in prayer turned the supplanter into a prevailing prince, and robed him with celestial grandeur. From that night he lives on the sacred page as one of the nobility of Heaven. Could not we, at least now and then, in these weary earthbound years, hedge about a single night for such enriching traffic with the skies? What, have we no sacred ambition? Are we deaf to the yearnings of Divine love? Yet, my brethren, for wealth and for science men will cheerfully quit their warm couches, and cannot we do it now and again for the love of God and the good of souls? Where is our zeal, our gratitude, our sincerity? I am ashamed while I thus upbraid both myself and you. May we often tarry at Jabbok, and cry with Jacob, as he grasped the angel—

> With thee all night I mean to stay,
> And wrestle till the break of day.

Surely, brethren, if we have given whole days to folly, we can afford a space for heavenly wisdom. Time was when we gave whole nights to chambering and wantonness, to dancing and the world's revelry; we did not tire then; we were chiding the sun that he rose so soon, and wishing the hours would lag awhile that we might delight in wilder merriment and perhaps deeper sin. Oh, wherefore, should we weary in heavenly employments? Why grow we weary in heavenly employments? Why grow we weary when asked to watch with our Lord? Up, sluggish heart. Jesus calls thee! Rise and go forth to meet the Heavenly Friend in the place where He manifests Himself."

We can never expect to grow in the likeness of our Lord unless we follow His example and give more time to communion with the Father. A revival of real praying would produce a spiritual revolution.

Bear up the hands that hang down, by faith and prayer; support the tottering knees. Have you any days of fasting and prayer? Storm the throne of grace and persevere there-in, and mercy will come down.

JOHN WESLEY

We must remember that the goal of prayer is the ear of God. Unless that is gained the prayer has utterly failed. The uttering of it may have kindled devotional feeling in our mind, the hearing of it may have comforted and strengthened the hearts of those with whom we have prayed, but if the prayer has not gained the heart of God, it has failed in its essential purpose.

A mere formalist can always pray so as to please himself. What has he to do but to open his book and read the prescribed words, or bow his knee and repeat such phrases as suggest themselves to his memory or his fancy? Like the Tartarian Praying Machine, give but the wind and the wheel, and the business is fully arranged. So much knee-bending and talking, and the prayer is done. The formalist's prayers are always good, or, rather, always bad, alike. But the living child of God never offers a prayer which pleases himself, his standard is above his attainments; he wonders that God listens to him, and though he knows he will be heard for Christ's sake, yet he accounts it a wonderful instance of condescending mercy that such poor prayers as his should ever reach the ears of the Lord God of Sabaoth.

C. H. SPURGEON

9

"ASK OF ME"

IT MAY BE SAID with emphasis that no lazy saint prays. Can there be a lazy saint? Can there be a prayerless saint? Does not slack praying cut short sainthood's crown and kingdom? Can there be a cowardly soldier? Can there be a saintly hypocrite? Can there be virtuous vice? It is only when these impossibilities are brought into being that we then can find a prayerless saint.

To go through the motion of praying is a dull business, though not a hard one. To say prayers in a decent, delicate way is not heavy work. But to really pray, to pray till hell feels the ponderous stroke, to pray till the iron gates of difficulty are opened, till the mountains of obstacles are removed, till the mists are exhaled and the clouds are lifted, and the sunshine of a cloudless day brightens—this is hard work, but it is God's work and man's best labor. Never was the toil of hand, head, and heart less spent in vain than when praying. It is hard to wait and press and pray and hear no voice, but stay till God answers. The joy of answered prayer is the joy of a travailing mother when a living child is born into the world, the joy of a slave whose chains have been burst asunder and to whom new life and liberty have just come.

A bird's-eye view of what has been accomplished by prayer shows what we lost when the dispensation of real prayer was substituted by Pharisaical pretense and sham;

77

it shows, too, how imperative is the need for holy men and women who will give themselves to earnest, Christlike praying.

It is not an easy thing to pray. Back of the praying there must lie all the conditions of prayer. These conditions are possible, but they are not to be seized on in a moment by the prayerless. Present they always may be to the faithful and holy, but they cannot exist in nor be met by a frivolous, negligent, laggard spirit. Prayer does not stand alone. It is not an isolated performance. Prayer stands in closest connection with all the duties of an ardent piety. It is the issuance of a character which is made up of the elements of a vigorous and commanding faith. Prayer honors God, acknowledges His being, exalts His power, adores His providence, secures His aid. A sneering half rationalism cries out against devotion, that it does nothing but pray. But to pray well is to do all things well. If it be true that devotion does nothing but pray, then it does nothing at all. To do nothing but pray fails to do the praying, for the antecedent, coincident, and subsequent conditions of prayer are but the sum of all the energized forces of a practical, working piety.

The possibilities of prayer run parallel with the promises of God. Prayer opens an outlet for the promises, removes the hindrances in the way of their execution, puts them into working order, and secures their gracious ends. More than this, prayer, like faith, obtains promises, enlarges their operation, and adds to the measure of their results. God's promises were to Abraham and to his seed, but many a barren womb and many a minor obstacle stood in the way of the fulfillment of these promises. But prayer removed them all, made a highway for the promises, added to the facility and speediness of their realization, and by prayer the promise shone bright and perfect in its execution.

The possibilities of prayer are found in its allying itself with the purposes of God, for God's purposes and man's praying are the combination of all potent and omnipotent forces. More than this, the possibilities of prayer are seen in the fact that it changes the purposes of God. It is in the very nature of prayer to plead and give directions. Prayer is not a negation. It is a positive force. It never rebels against the will of God, never comes into conflict with that will, but it is evident that it does seek to change God's purpose. Christ said, "The cup which the Father hath given me, shall I not drink it?" (Jn 18:11), and yet He had prayed that very night, "Father, if thou be willing, remove this cup from me" (Lk 22:42). Paul sought to change the purposes of God about the thorn in his flesh. God's purposes were fixed to destroy Israel, and the prayer of Moses changed the purposes of God and saved Israel. In the time of the judges, Israelites were apostate and greatly oppressed. They repented and cried unto God, and He said: "Ye have forsaken me, and served other gods: wherefore I will save you no more." But they humbled themselves and put away their strange gods, and God's "soul was grieved for the misery of Israel" (Judg 10:13-16), and He sent them deliverance by Jephthah.

God sent Isaiah to say to Hezekiah, "Set thine house in order; for thou shalt die, and not live" (Is 38:1); and Hezekiah prayed, and God sent Isaiah back to say, "I have heard thy prayer, I have seen thy tears: behold I will add unto thy days fifteen years" (v. 5).

"Yet forty days and Nineveh shall be overthrown" (Jon 3:4) was God's message by Jonah. But Nineveh cried mightily to God, and "God repented of the evil which he said he would do unto them; and he did it not" (v. 10).

The possibilities of prayer are seen from the divers conditions it reaches and the diverse ends it secures. Elijah prayed over a dead child, and it came to life; Elisha did the same thing; Christ prayed at Lazarus's grave, and Lazarus came forth. Peter knelt down and prayed beside dead Dorcas, and she opened her eyes and sat up, and Peter presented her alive to the distressed company. Paul prayed for Publius and healed him. Jacob's praying changed Esau's murderous hate into the kisses of the tenderest brotherly embrace. God gave Jacob and Esau to Rebecca because Isaac prayed for her. Joseph was the child of Rachel's prayers. Hannah's praying gave Samuel to Israel. John the Baptist was given to Elisabeth, barren and past age as she was, in answer to the prayer of Zacharias. Elisha's praying brought famine or harvest to Israel; as he prayed so it was. Ezra's praying carried the Spirit of God in heartbreaking conviction to the entire city of Jerusalem, and brought them in tears of repentance back to God. Isaiah's praying carried the shadow of the sun back ten degrees on the dial of Ahaz.

In answer to Hezekiah's praying, an angel slew 185,000 of Sennacherib's army in one night. Daniel's praying opened to him the vision of prophecy, helped him to administer the affairs of a mighty kingdom, and sent an angel to shut the lions' mouths. The angel was sent to Cornelius, and the Gospel opened through him to the Gentile world, because he was told, "Thy prayers and thine alms are gone up for a memorial before God" (Ac 10:4).

"And what shall I more say? For the time will fail me if I tell of Gideon, Barak, Samson, Jephthah; of David and Samuel and the prophets" (Heb 11:32); of Paul, Peter, John, the apostles, and the holy company of saints,

reformers, and martyrs, who, through praying, "subdued
kingdoms, wrought righteousness, obtained promises,
stopped the mouths of lions, quenched the power of fire,
escaped the edge of the sword, from weakness were made
strong, waxed mighty in war, turned to flight armies of
aliens" (vv. 33-34).

Prayer puts God in the matter with commanding force:
"Ask me of the things to come: concerning my sons," says
God, "and concerning the work of my hands, command
ye me" (Is 45:11). We are charged in God's Word "always to pray . . . in everything by prayer . . . continuing
instant in prayer," to "pray everywhere . . . praying always." The promise is as illimitable as the command is
comprehensive. "All things whatsoever ye shall ask in
prayer, believing, ye shall receive . . . whatever ye shall
ask, . . . if ye shall ask anything." "Ye shall ask what ye
will and it shall be done unto you. . . . Whatsoever ye ask
the Father he will give it to you." If there is anything not
involved in "All things whatsoever," or not found in the
phrase "Ask anything," then these things may be left out
of prayer. Language could not cover a wider range nor
involve more fully all minutiae. These statements are
only samples of the all-comprehending possibilities of
prayer under the promises of God to those who meet the
conditions of right praying.

These passages, though, give only a general outline of
the immense regions over which prayer extends its sway.
Beyond these the effects of prayer reaches and secures
good from regions which cannot be traversed by language
or thought. Paul exhausted language and thought in
praying; but, conscious of necessities not covered and
realms of good not reached, he covers these impenetrable
and undiscovered regions by this general plea: "unto him

that is able to do exceeding abundantly above all that we ask or think, according to the power that worketh in us" (Eph 3:20). The promise is, "Call unto me, and I will answer thee, and will show thee great things, and difficult which thou knowest not" (Jer 33:3).

James declares that "the supplication of a righteous man availeth much" (Ja 5:16). How much he could not tell, but he illustrates it by the power of Old Testament praying to stir up New Testament saints to imitate by the fervor and influence of their praying the holy men of old, and duplicate and surpass the power of their praying. "Elijah," he says, "was a man of like passions with us, and he prayed fervently that it might not rain; and it rained not on the earth for three years and six months. And he prayed again; and the heaven gave rain, and the earth brought forth her fruit" (vv. 17-18).

In the Revelation of John the whole lower order of God's creation and His providential government, the Church and the angelic world, are in the attitude of waiting on the efficiency of the prayers of the saintly ones on earth to carry on the various interests of earth and heaven. The angel takes the fire kindled by prayer and casts it earthward, "and there followed thunders, and voices, and lightnings, and an earthquake" (Rev 8:5). Prayer is the force which creates all these alarms, stirs, and throes. "Ask of me," says God to His Son, and to the Church of His Son, "and I will give thee the nations for thine inheritance, and the uttermost parts of the earth for thy possession" (Ps 2:8).

The men who have done mighty things for God have always been mighty in prayer, have well understood the possibilities of prayer, and made the most of these possibilities. The Son of God, the first of all and the mightiest of all, has shown us the all-potent and far-reaching possibilities of prayer. Paul was mighty for God because he knew how to use, and how to get others to use, the mighty spiritual forces of prayer.

The seraphim, burning, sleepless, adoring, is the figure of prayer. It is resistless in its ardor; it is devoted and tireless. There are hindrances to prayer that nothing but pure, intense flame can surmount. There are toils, outlays, and endurance which nothing but the strongest, most ardent flame can abide. Prayer may be low-tongued, but it cannot be cold-tongued. Its words may be few, but they must be on fire. Its feelings may not be impetuous, but they must be white with heat. It is the effectual, fervent prayer that influences God.

God's house is the house of prayer; God's work is the work of prayer. It is the zeal for God's house and the zeal for God's work that makes God's house glorious and His work abide.

When the prayer chambers of saints are closed or are entered casually or coldly, then Church rulers are secular, fleshly, and materialized; spiritual character sinks to a low level, and the ministry becomes restrained and enfeebled. *Prayer ministry*

When prayer fails, the world prevails. When prayer fails, the Church loses its divine characteristics, its divine power; the Church is swallowed up by a proud ecclesiasticism, and the world scoffs at its obvious impotence. *Prayer Church*

I look upon all the four Gospels as thoroughly genuine, for there is in them the reflection of a greatness which emanated from the person of Jesus and which was of as Divine a kind as ever was seen on earth.

GOETHE

There are no possibilities, no necessity for prayerless praying, a heartless performance, a senseless routine, a dead habit, a hasty, careless performance—it justifies nothing. Prayerless praying has no life, gives no life, is dead, breathes out death. Not a battle-axe but a child's toy, for play not for service. Prayerless praying does not come up to the importance and aims of a recreation. Prayerless praying is only a weight, an impediment in the hour of struggle, of intense conflict, a call to retreat in the moment of battle and victory.

SOURCE UNKNOWN

10

DIFFICULTIES TO A LIFE
OF PRAYER

WHY DO WE NOT PRAY? What are the hindrances to prayer? This is not a curious or trivial question. It goes not only to the whole matter of our praying, but to the whole matter of our religion. Religion is bound to decline when praying is hindered. That which hinders praying, hinders religion. He who is too busy to pray will be too busy to live a holy life.

Other duties become pressing and absorbing and crowd out prayer. "Choked to death" would be the coroner's verdict in many cases of dead praying if an inquest could be secured on this dire, spiritual calamity. This way of hindering prayer becomes so natural, so easy, so innocent that it comes on us all unawares. If we will allow our praying to be crowded out, it will always be done. Satan had rather we let the grass grow on the path to our prayer chamber than anything else. A closed chamber of prayer means "gone out of business religiously" or, what is worse, made an assignment and carrying on our religion in some other name than God's and to somebody else's glory. God's glory is only secured in the business of religion by carrying that religion on with a large capital of prayer. The apostles understood this when they declared that their time must not be employed in even the sacred duties of alms-giving; they must, they said, "continue stedfastly

in prayer, and in the ministry of the word" (Ac 6:4),
prayer being put first with them and the ministry of the
Word having its efficiency and life from prayer.

The process of hindering prayer by crowding it out is
simple and goes by advancing stages. First, prayer is
hurried through. Unrest and agitation, fatal to all devout
exercises, come in. Then the time is shortened, and relish
for the exercise palls. Then it is crowded into a corner
and depends on the fragments of time for its exercise. Its
value depreciates. The duty has lost its importance. It
no longer commands respect nor brings benefit. It has
fallen out of estimate, out of the heart, out of the habits,
out of the life. We cease to pray and cease to live spiritually.

There is no stay to the desolating floods of worldliness
and business and cares except prayer. Christ meant this
when He charged us to watch and pray. There is no pio-
neering corps for the Gospel but prayer. Paul knew that
when he declared he was "night and day praying exceed-
ingly that we may see your face, and may perfect that
which is lacking in your faith" (1 Th 3:10). There is no
arriving at a high state of grace without much praying
and no staying in those high altitudes without great praying. Epaphras knew this when he was "always striving . . .
in his prayers" for the Colossian church, that they "may
stand perfect and fully assured in all the will of God"
(Col 4:12).

The only way to preserve our praying from being hindered is to estimate prayer at its true and great value.
Estimate it as Daniel did, who, when he "knew that the
writing was signed, he went into his house; (now his
windows were open, . . . toward Jerusalem;) and he
kneeled upon his knees three times a day, and prayed,

and gave thanks before his God, as he did aforetime"
(Dan 6:10). Put praying into the high values as Daniel
did, above place, honor, ease, wealth, life. Put praying
into the habits as Daniel did. "As he did aforetime" has
much in it to give firmness and fidelity in the hour of
trial; much is in it to remove hindrances and master op-
posing circumstances.

One of Satan's wiliest tricks is to destroy the best by the
good. Business and other duties are good, but we are so
filled with these that they crowd out and destroy the best.
Prayer holds the citadel for God; if Satan can by any
means weaken prayer, he is a gainer; and when prayer is
dead the citadel is taken. We must keep prayer as the
faithful sentinel keeps guard, with sleepless vigilance.
We must not keep it half-starved and feeble as a baby, but
we must keep it in giant strength. Our prayer chamber
should have our freshest strength, our calmest time, its
hours unfettered, without obtrusion, without haste. Private place and plenty of time are the life of prayer. To
kneel upon our knees three times a day and pray and give
thanks before God as we did "aforetime," is the very heart
and soul of religion, and makes men, like Daniel, of "an
excellent spirit" (Dan 5:12) "greatly beloved" (9:23).

The greatness of prayer, involving as it does the whole
man, in the intensest form, is not realized without spiritual discipline. This makes it hard work; and before this
exacting and consuming effort, our spiritual sloth or feebleness stands abashed.

The simplicity of prayer, its childlike elements, form
a great obstacle to true praying. Intellect gets in the way
of the heart. Only the child spirit is the spirit of prayer.
It is no holiday occupation to make the man a child again.
In song, in poetry, in memory he may wish himself a

child again, but in prayer he must be a child again in reality, at his mother's knee, artless, sweet, intense, direct, trustful, with no shade of doubt, no temper to be denied. He must have a desire which burns and consumes which can only be voiced by a cry. It is no easy work to have this childlike spirit of prayer.

If praying were but an hour in the closet, difficulties would face and hinder even that hour; but praying is the whole life preparing for the closet. How difficult it is to cover home and business, all the sweets and all the bitters of life, with the holy atmosphere of the closet! A holy life is the only preparation for prayer. It is just as difficult to pray as it is to live a holy life. In this we find a wall of exclusion built around our closets; men do not love holy praying, because they do not love and will not do holy living. Montgomery sets forth the difficulties of true praying when he declares the sublimity and simplicity of prayer.

> Prayer is the simplest form of speech
>   That infant lips can try.
> Prayer is the sublimest strains that reach
>   The Majesty on high.

This is not only good poetry, but a profound truth as to the loftiness and simplicity of prayer. There are great difficulties in reaching the exalted, angelic strains of prayer. The difficulty of coming down to the simplicity of infant lips is not much less.

Prayer in the Old Testament is called wrestling. Conflict, skill, and strenuous, exhaustive effort are involved. In the New Testament we have the terms striving, laboring fervently, fervent, effectual, and agony, all indicating intense effort put forth and difficulties overcome. We, in our praises sing:

> What various hindrances we meet
> In coming to a mercy seat.

We also have learned that the gracious results secured by prayer are generally proportioned to the outlay in removing the hindrances which obstruct our soul's high communion with God.

Christ spake a parable to this end, that men ought always to pray and not to faint. The parable of the importunate widow teaches the difficulties in praying, how they are to be surmounted, and the happy results which follow from valorous praying. Difficulties will always obstruct the way to the closet as long as it remains true

> That Satan trembles when he sees
> The weakest saint upon his knees.

Courageous faith is made stronger and purer by mastering difficulties. These difficulties but couch the eye of faith to the glorious prize which is to be won by the successful wrestler in prayer. Men must not faint in the contest of prayer, but to this high and holy work they must give themselves, defying the difficulties in the way, and experiencing more than an angel's happiness in the results. Luther said: "To have prayed well is to have studied well." More than that, to have prayed well is to have fought well. To have prayed well is to have lived well. To pray well is to die well.

Prayer is a rare gift, not a popular, ready gift. Prayer is not the fruit of natural talents; it is the product of faith, of holiness, of deeply spiritual character. Men learn to pray as they learn to love. Perfection in simplicity, in humility, in faith—these form its chief ingredients. Novices in these graces are not adept in prayer. It cannot be seized upon by untrained hands; graduates in heaven's highest school of art can alone touch its finest keys, raise its sweetest, highest notes. Fine material and fine finish are requisite. Master workmen are required, for mere journeymen cannot execute the work of prayer.

The spirit of prayer should rule our spirits and our conduct. The spirit of the prayer chamber must control our lives or the closet hour will be dull and sapless. Always praying in spirit, always acting in the spirit of praying—these make our praying strong. The spirit of every moment is that which imparts strength to the closet communion. It is what we are out of the closet which gives victory or brings defeat to the closet. If the spirit of the world prevails in our non-closet hours, the spirit of the world will prevail in our closet hours, and that will be a vain and idle farce.

We must live for God out of the closet if we would meet God in the closet. We must bless God by praying lives if we would have God's blessing in the closet. We must do God's will in our lives if we would have God's ear in the closet. We must listen to God's voice in public if we would have God listen to our voice in private. God must have our hearts out of the closet if we would have God's presence in the closet. If we would have God in the closet, God must have us out of the closet. There is no way of praying to God but by living to God. The closet is not a confessional, simply, but the hour of holy communion and high and sweet fellowship and of intense intercession.

Men would pray better if they lived better. They would

get more from God if they lived more obedient and well-pleasing to God. We would have more strength and time for the divine work of intercession if we did not have to expend so much strength and time settling up old scores and paying our delinquent taxes. Our spiritual liabilities are so greatly in excess of our spiritual assets that our closet time is spent in taking out a decree of bankruptcy instead of being the time of great spiritual wealth for us and for others. Our closets are too much like the sign, Closed for Repairs.

John said of primitive Christian praying, "Whatsoever we ask we receive of him, because we keep his commandments and do the things that are pleasing in his sight" (1 Jn 3:22). We should note what illimitable grounds were covered, what illimitable gifts were received by their strong praying: "Whatsoever"—how comprehensive the range and reception of mighty praying, how suggestive the reasons for the ability to pray and to have prayers answered. Obedience, but more than mere obedience, doing the things which please God well. They went to their closets made strong by their strict obedience and loving fidelity to God in their conduct. Their lives were not only true and obedient, but they were thinking about things above obedience, searching for and doing things to make God glad. These can come with eager step and radiant countenance to meet their Father in the closet, not simply to be forgiven, but to be approved and to receive.

It makes a lot of difference whether we come to God as a criminal or a child, to be pardoned or to be approved, to settle scores or to be embraced, for punishment or for favor. Our praying to be strong must be buttressed by holy living. The name of Christ must be honored by our lives before He will honor our intercessions. The life of faith perfects the prayer of faith.

Our lives not only give color to our praying, but they give body to it as well. Bad living makes bad praying. We pray feebly because we live feebly. The stream of praying cannot rise higher than the fountain of living. The closet force is made up of the energy which flows from the confluent streams of living. The feebleness of living throws its faintness into closet homes. We cannot talk to God strongly when we have not lived for God strongly. The closet cannot be made holy to God when the life has not been holy to God. The Word of God emphasizes our conduct as giving value to our praying. "Then shalt thou call, and Jehovah will answer; thou shalt cry, and he shall say, Here I am. If thou take away from the midst of thee the yoke, the putting forth of the finger, and speaking wickedly (Is 58:9).

Men are to pray "lifting up holy hands, without wrath and disputing" (1 Ti 2:8). We are to pass the time of our sojourning here in fear if we would call on the Father. We cannot divorce praying from conduct. "Whatsoever we ask we receive of him, because we keep his commandments and do the things that are pleasing in his sight" (1 Jn 3:22). "Ye ask and receive not, because ye ask amiss, that ye may spend it in your pleasures" (Ja 4:3). The injunction of Christ, "Watch and pray" (Mt 26:41), is to cover and guard conduct that we may come to our closets with all the force secured by a vigilant guard over our lives.

Our religion breaks down most often and most sadly in our conduct. Beautiful theories are marred by ugly lives. The most difficult as well as the most impressive point in piety is to live it. Our praying suffers as much

as our religion from bad living. Preachers were charged
in primitive times to preach by their lives or preach not
at all. So Christians everywhere ought to be charged to
pray by their lives or pray not at all. Of course, the prayer
of repentance is acceptable. But repentance means to
quit doing wrong and learn to do well. A repentance
which does not produce a change in conduct is a sham.
Praying which does not result in pure conduct is a delusion. We have missed the whole office and virtue of praying if it does not rectify conduct. It is in the very nature
of things that we must quit praying or quit bad conduct.
Cold, dead praying may exist with bad conduct, but cold,
dead praying is no praying in God's esteem. Our praying
advances in power as it rectifies the life. A life growing
in its purity and devotion will be a more prayerful life.

The pity is that so much of our praying is without
object or aim. It is without purpose. How much praying
there is by men and women who never abide in Christ.
It is hasty praying, sweet praying full of sentiment, pleasing praying, but not backed by a life wedded to Christ.
Popular praying! How much of this praying is from unsanctified hearts and unhallowed lips! Prayers spring into
life under the influence of some great excitement, by some
pressing emergency, through some popular clamor, some
great peril. But the conditions of prayer are not there.
We rush into God's presence and try to link Him to our
cause, inflame Him with our passions, move Him by our
peril. All things are to be prayed for, but with clean
hands, with absolute deference to God's will and abiding
in Christ. Prayerless praying by lips and hearts untrained
to prayer, by lives out of harmony with Jesus Christ;
prayerless praying, which has the form and motion of
prayer but is without the true heart of prayer, never

moves God to an answer. It is of such praying that James
says: "Ye have not, because ye ask not. Ye ask, and receive
not, because ye ask amiss" (Ja 4:2-3) .

The two great evils are not asking, and asking in a
wrong way. Perhaps the greater evil is wrong asking, for
it has in it the show of duty done, of praying when there
has been no praying, which is a deceit, a fraud, a sham.
The times of the most praying are not really the times of
the best praying. The Pharisees prayed much, but they
were actuated by vanity; their praying was the symbol of
their hypocrisy by which they made God's house of prayer
a den of robbers. Theirs was praying on state occasions—
mechanical, perfunctory, professional, beautiful in words,
fragrant in sentiment, well-ordered, well-received by the
ears that heard—but utterly devoid of every element of
real prayer.

The conditions of prayer are well-ordered and clear:
abiding in Christ, in His name. One of the first necessities, if we are to grasp the infinite possibilities of prayer,
is to get rid of prayerless praying. It is often beautiful in
words and in execution; it has the drapery of prayer in
rich and costly form, but it lacks the soul of praying. We
fall so easily into the habit of prayerless service, of merely
filling a program.

If men only prayed on all occasions and in every place
where they go through the motion! If only there were
holy inflamed hearts back of all these beautiful words and
gracious forms! If only there were always uplifted hearts
in these erect men who are uttering flawless but vain
words before God! If only there were always reverent
bended hearts when bended knees are uttering words
before God to please men's ears!

There is nothing that will preserve the life of prayer—

its vigor, sweetness, obligations, seriousness, and value—
so much as a deep conviction that prayer is an approach
to God, a pleading with God, an asking of God. Reality
will then be in it; reverence will then be in the attitude,
in the place, and in the air. Faith will draw, kindle, and
open. Formality and deadness cannot live in this high
and all-serious home of the soul.

Prayerless praying lacks the essential element of true
praying; it is not based on desire and is devoid of earnestness and faith. Desire burdens the chariot of prayer,
and faith drives its wheels. Prayerless praying has no
burden because there is no sense of need; there is no ardor
because there is none of the vision, strength, or glow of
faith. There is no mighty pressure to prayer, no holding
on to God with the deathless, despairing grasp, "I will
not let thee go, except thou bless me" (Gen 32:26). There
is no utter self-abandonment, lost in the throes of a des-
perate, pertinacious, and consuming plea: "Yet now if
thou wilt forgive their sin—if not, blot me, I pray thee,
out of thy book" (Ex 32:32), or, "Give me Scotland, or
I die." Prayerless praying stakes nothing on the issue, for
it has nothing to stake. It comes with empty hands, indeed, but they are listless hands as well as empty. They
have never learned the lesson of empty hands clinging to
the cross; this lesson to them has no form nor comeliness.

Prayerless praying has no heart in its praying. The
lack of heart deprives praying of its reality and makes it
an empty and unfit vessel. Heart, soul, and life must be
in our praying; the heavens must feel the force of our
crying and must be brought into oppressed sympathy for
our bitter and needy state. A need that oppresses us, and
has no relief but in our crying to God, must voice our
praying.

Prayerless praying is insincere. It has no honesty at heart. We name in words what we do not want in heart. Our prayers give formal utterance to the things for which our hearts are not only not hungry, but for which they really have no taste. I once heard an eminent and saintly preacher, now in heaven, come abruptly and sharply on a congregation that had just risen from prayer, with the question and statement, "What did you pray for? If God should take hold of you and shake you, and demand what you prayed for, you could not tell Him to save your life what the prayer was that has just died from your lips." So it always is; prayerless praying has neither memory nor heart. A mere form, a heterogeneous mass, an insipid compound, a mixture thrown together for sound and to fill up, but with neither heart nor aim, is prayerless praying. A dry routine, a dreary drudge, a dull and heavy task is this prayerless praying.

But prayerless praying is much worse than either task or drudge. It divorces praying from living; it utters its words against the world, but with heart and life runs into the world; it prays for humility, but nurtures pride; prays for self-denial while indulging the flesh. Nothing exceeds true praying in gracious results, but it is better not to pray at all than to pray prayerless prayers, for they are but sinning, and the worst of sinning is to sin on our knees.

The prayer habit is a good habit, but praying by dint of habit only is a very bad habit. This kind of praying is not conditioned after God's order, nor generated by God's power. It is not only a waste, a perversion, and a delusion, but it is a prolific source of unbelief. Prayerless praying gets no results. God is not reached, self is not helped. It is better not to pray at all than to secure no results from praying. Better for the one who prays, better for others. Men hear of the prodigious results which are to be secured by prayer, the matchless good promised in God's Word to prayer. These keen-eyed worldings or timid little-faith ones mark the great discrepancy between the results promised, not results realized, and are led necessarily to doubt the truth and worth of that which is so big in promise and so beggarly in results. Religion and God are dishonored, while doubt and unbelief are strengthened by much asking and no getting.

In contrast with this, what a mighty force prayerful praying is! Real prayer helps God and man. God's Kingdom is advanced by it. The greatest good comes to man by it. Prayer can do anything that God can do. The pity is that we do not believe this as we ought, and we do not put it to the test.

11

PRAYER CAN DO ANYTHING THAT GOD CAN DO

THE PRECEDING CHAPTER closed with the statement that prayer can do anything that God can do. It is a tremendous statement to make, but it is a statement borne out by history and experience. If we are abiding in Christ—and if we abide in Him we are living in obedience to His holy will—and approach God in His name, then there lie open before us the infinite resources of the divine treasure-house.

The man who truly prays gets from God many things denied to the prayerless man. The aim of all real praying is to get the thing prayed for, as the child's cry for bread has for its end the getting of bread. This view removes prayer clean out of the sphere of religious performances. Prayer is not acting a part or going through religious motions. Prayer is neither official nor formal nor ceremonial, but direct, hearty, intense. Prayer is not religious work which must be gone through, which avails because it is well done. Prayer is the helpless and needy child crying to the compassion of the Father's heart and the bounty and power of a Father's hand. The answer is as sure to come as the Father's heart can be touched and the Father's hand can be moved.

The object of asking is to receive. The aim of seeking is to find. The purpose of knocking is to arouse attention

98

and get in, and this is Christ's iterated and reiterated asseveration that the prayer without doubt will be answered, its end without doubt secured. Not by some roundabout way, but by getting the very thing asked for.

The value of prayer does not lie in the number of prayers, or the length of prayers, but its value is found in the great truth that we are privileged by our relations to God to unburden our desires and make our requests known to God, and He will relieve by granting our petitions. The child asks because the parent is in the habit of granting the child's requests. As the children of God we need something and we need it badly, and we go to God for it. Neither the Bible nor the child of God knows anything of that half-infidel declaration that we are to answer our own prayers. God answers prayer. The true Christian does not pray to stir himself up, but his prayer is the stirring up of himself to take hold of God. The heart of faith knows nothing of that specious skepticism which stays the steps of prayer and chills its ardor by whispering that prayer does not affect God.

D. L. Moody used to tell a story of a little child whose father and mother had died, and who was taken into another family. The first night she asked whether she could pray as she used to do. They said: "Oh, yes!" So she knelt down and prayed as her mother had taught her; and when that was ended, she added a little prayer of her own: "O God, make these people as kind to me as Father and Mother were." Then she paused and looked up, as if expecting the answer, and then added: "Of course You will." How sweetly simple was that little one's faith! She expected God to answer and "do," and "of course" she got her request, and that is the spirit in which God invites us to approach Him.

In contrast to that incident is the story told of the quaint Yorkshire class leader, Daniel Quorm, who was visiting a friend. One forenoon he came to the friend and said, "I am sorry you have met with such a great disappointment."

"Why, no," said the man, "I have not met with any disappointment."

"Yes," said Daniel, "you were expecting something remarkable today."

"What do you mean?" said the friend.

"Why, you prayed that you might be kept sweet and gentle all day long. And, by the way things have been going, I see you have been greatly disappointed."

"Oh," said the man, "I thought you meant something particular."

Prayer is mighty in its operations, and God never disappoints those who put their trust and confidence in Him. They may have to wait long for the answer, and they may not live to see it, but the prayer of faith never misses its object.

"A friend of mine in Cincinnati had preached his sermon and sank back in his chair, when he felt impelled to make another appeal," says Dr. J. Wilbur Chapman. "A boy at the back of the church lifted his hand. My friend left the pulpit and went down to him, and said, 'Tell me about yourself.' The boy said, 'I live in New York. I am a prodigal. I have disgraced my father's name and broken my mother's heart. I ran away and told them I would never come back until I became a Christian or they brought me home dead.' That night there went from Cincinnati a letter telling his father and mother that their boy had turned to God.

"Seven days later, in a black-bordered envelope, a reply

came which read: 'My dear boy, when I got the news that
you had received Jesus Christ the sky was overcast; your
father was dead.' Then the letter went on to tell how the
father had prayed for his prodigal boy with his last
breath, and concluded, 'You are a Christian tonight because your old father would not let you go.' "

A fourteen-year-old boy was given a task by his father.
A group of boys came along just then and lured the boy
away with them, and so the work went undone. But the
father came home that evening and said, "Frank, did you
do the work that I gave you?" "Yes, sir," said Frank. He
told an untruth; and his father knew it, but said nothing.
It troubled the boy, but he went to bed as usual. Next
morning his mother said to him, "Your father did not
sleep all last night."

"Why didn't he sleep?" asked Frank.

His mother said, "He spent the whole night praying
for you."

This sent the arrow into his heart. He was deeply con-
victed of his sin and knew no rest until he had gotten
right with God. Long afterward, when the boy became
Bishop Warne, he said that his decision for Christ came
from his father's prayer that night. He saw his father
keeping his lonely and sorrowful vigil praying for his boy,
and it broke his heart. He said, "I can never be sufficient-
ly grateful to him for that prayer."

An evangelist, much used of God, has put on record
that he commenced a series of meetings in a little church
of about twenty members who were very cold and dead,
and much divided. A little prayer meeting was kept up
by two or three women. "I preached, and closed at eight
o'clock," he says. "There was no one to speak or pray.
The next evening one man spoke.

"The next morning I rode six miles to a minister's study and kneeled in prayer. I went back and said to the little church:

" 'If you can make out enough to board me, I will stay until God opens the windows of Heaven. God has promised to bless these means, and I believe He will.'

"Within ten days there were so many anxious souls that I met one hundred and fifty of them at a time in an inquiry meeting, while Christians were praying in another house of worship. Several hundred, I think, were converted. It is safe to believe God."

A mother asked the late John B. Gough to visit her son to win him to Christ. Gough found the young man's mind full of skeptical notions and impervious to argument. Finally, the young man was asked to pray just once for light. He replied: "I do not know anything perfect to whom or to which I could pray."

"How about your mother's love?" said the orator. "Isn't that perfect? Hasn't she always stood by you, and been ready to take you in, and care for you, when even your father had really kicked you out?"

The young man choked with emotion, and said, "Ye-s, sir; that is so."

"Then pray to Love—it will help you. Will you promise?" He promised. That night the young man prayed in the privacy of his room. He knelt down, closed his eyes, and struggling a moment, uttered the words: "O Love." Instantly, as by a flash of lightning, the old Bible text came to him: "God is love," and he said brokenly, "O God!" Then another flash of divine truth, and a voice said, "God so loved the world, that he gave his only begotten Son"; and there, instantly, he exclaimed, "O Christ, Thou incarnation of Divinest love, show me light and truth." It was all over. He was in the light of the most perfect peace. He ran downstairs, adds the narrator of this incident, and told his mother that he was saved. That young man is today an eloquent minister of Jesus Christ.

A water famine was threatened in Hakodate, Japan. Miss Dickerson, of the Methodist Episcopal Girls' School, saw the water supply growing less daily, and in one of the fall months appealed to the board in New York for help. There was no money on hand, and nothing was done. Miss Dickerson inquired the cost of putting down an artesian well, but found the expense too great to be undertaken. On the evening of December 31, when the water was almost exhausted, the teachers and the older pupils met to pray for water, though they had no idea how their prayer was to be answered. A couple of days later a letter was received in the New York office which ran something like this: "Philadelphia, January 1st. It is six o'clock in the morning of New Year's Day. All the other members of the family are asleep, but I was awakened with a strange impression that someone, somewhere, is in need of money which the Lord wants me to supply." Enclosed was a check for an amount which just covered the cost of the artesian well and the piping of the water into the school buildings.

"I have seen God's hand stretched out to heal among the heathen in as mighty wonder-working power as in apostolic times," a well-known minister once said to me. "I was preaching to two thousand famine orphan girls, at Kedgaum, India, at Ramabai's Mukti (salvation) Mission. A swarm of serpents as venomous and deadly as the reptile that smote Paul, suddenly raided the walled grounds, 'sent of Satan,' Ramabai said, and several of her

most beautiful and faithful Christian girls were smitten
by them, two of them bitten twice. I saw four of the very
flower of her flock in convulsions at once, unconscious
and apparently in the agonies of death.

"Ramabai believes the Bible with an implicit and
obedient faith. Three of us missionaries were there. She
said: 'We will do just what the Bible says. I want you to
minister for their healing according to James 5:14-18.'
She led the way into the dormitory where her girls were
lying in spasms, and we laid our hands upon their heads
and prayed, and anointed them with oil in the name of
the Lord. Each of them was healed as soon as anointed
and sat up and sang with faces shining. That miracle and
marvel among the heathen mightily confirmed the word
of the Lord, and was a profound and overpowering proc-
lamation of God."

Some years ago, the record of a wonderful work of grace
in connection with one of the stations of the China Inland Mission attracted a good deal of attention. Both the
number and spiritual character of the converts had been
far greater than at other stations where the consecration
of the missionaries had been just as great as at the more
fruitful place.

This rich harvest of souls remained a mystery until
Hudson Taylor on a visit to England discovered the
secret. At the close of one of his addresses, a gentleman
came forward to make his acquaintance. In the conversation which followed, Mr. Taylor was surprised at the
accurate knowledge the man possessed concerning this
inland China station. "But how is it," Mr. Taylor asked,
"that you are so conversant with the conditions of that
work?" "Oh!" he replied. "The missionary there and I
are old college-mates; for years we have regularly corre-

sponded; he has sent me names of enquirers and converts, and these I have daily taken to God in prayer."

At last the secret was found! A praying man at home, praying definitely, praying daily, for specific cases among the heathen. That is the real intercessory missionary.

Hudson Taylor himself, as all the world knows, was a man who knew how to pray and whose praying was blessed with fruitful answers. In the story of his life, told by Dr. and Mrs. Howard Taylor, we find page after page aglow with answered prayer. On his way out to China for the first time in 1853, when he was only twenty-one years of age, he had a definite answer to prayer that was a great encouragement to his faith. "They had just come through the Dampier Strait, but were not yet out of sight of the islands. Usually a breeze would spring up after sunset and last until about dawn. The utmost use was made of it, but during the day they lay still with flapping sails, often drifting back and losing a good deal of the advantage gained at night." The story continues in Hudson Taylor's own words:

"This happened notably on one occasion when we were in dangerous proximity to the north of New Guinea. Saturday night had brought us to a point some thirty miles off the land, and during the Sunday morning service, which was held on deck, I could not fail to see that the Captain looked troubled and frequently went over to the side of the ship. When the service was ended I learnt from him the cause. A four-knot current was carrying us toward some sunken reefs, and we were already so near that it seemed improbable that we should get through the afternoon in safety. After dinner, the long boat was put out and all hands endeavoured, without success, to turn the ship's head from the shore.

"After standing together on the deck for some time in silence, the Captain said to me:

" 'Well, we have done everything that can be done. We can only await the result.'

"A thought occurred to me, and I replied: 'No, there is one thing we have not done yet.'

" 'What is that?' he queried.

" 'Four of us on board are Christians. Let us each retire to his own cabin, and in agreed prayer ask the Lord to give us immediately a breeze. He can as easily send it now as at sunset.'

"The Captain complied with this proposal. I went and spoke to the other two men, and after prayer with the carpenter, we all four retired to wait upon God. I had a good but very brief season in prayer, and then felt so satisfied that our request was granted that I could not continue asking, and very soon went up again on deck. The first officer, a godless man, was in charge. I went over and asked him to let down the clews or corners of the mainsail, which had been drawn up in order to lessen the useless flapping of the sail against the rigging.

" 'What would be the good of that?' he answered roughly.

"I told him we had been asking a wind from God; that it was coming immediately; and we were so near the reef by this time that there was not a minute to lose.

"With an oath and a look of contempt, he said he would rather see a wind than hear of it.

"But while he was speaking I watched his eye, following it up to the royal, and there, sure enough, the corner of the topmost sail was beginning to tremble in the breeze.

" 'Don't you see the wind is coming? Look at the royal!' I exclaimed.

" 'No, it is only a cat's paw,' he rejoined (a mere puff of wind).

" 'Cat's paw or not,' I cried, 'pray let down the mainsail and give us the benefit.'

"This he was not slow to do. In another minute the heavy tread of the men on deck brought up the Captain from his cabin to see what was the matter. The breeze had indeed come! In a few minutes we were ploughing our way at six or seven knots an hour through the water . . . and though the wind was sometimes unsteady, we did not altogether lose it until after passing the Pelew Islands.

"Thus God encouraged me," adds this praying saint, "ere landing on China's shores to bring every variety of need to Him in prayer, and to expect that He would honor the name of the Lord Jesus and give the help each emergency required."

In an address at Cambridge some time ago (reported in *The Life of Faith*, April 3, 1912), Mr. S. D. Gordon told in his own inimitable way the story of a man in his own country, to illustrate from real life the fact of the reality of prayer, and that it is not mere talking.

"This man," said Mr. Gordon, "came of an old New England family, a bit farther back an English family. He was a giant in size, and a keen man mentally, and a university-trained man. He had gone out West to live, and represented a prominent district in our House of Congress, answering to your House of Commons. He was a prominent leader there. He was reared in a Christian family, but he was a skeptic, and used to lecture against Christianity. He told me he was fond, in his lectures, of proving, as he thought, conclusively, that there was no God. That was the type of his infidelity.

"One day he told me he was sitting in the Lower House
of Congress. It was at the time of a Presidential Election,
and when party feeling ran high. One would have thought
that was the last place where a man would be likely to
think about spiritual things. He said: 'I was sitting in my
seat in that crowded House and that heated atmosphere,
when a feeling came to me that the God, whose existence
I thought I could successfully disprove, was just there
above me, looking down on me, and that He was displeased with me, and with the way I was doing. I said to
myself, 'This is ridiculous, I guess I've been working too
hard. I'll go and get a good meal and take a long walk
and shake myself, and see if that will take this feeling
away.' He got his extra meal, took a walk, and came back
to his seat, but the impression would not be shaken off
that God was there and was displeased with him. He went
for a walk, day after day, but could never shake the feeling
off. Then he went back to his constituency in his State,
he said, to arrange matters there. He had the ambition
to be the Governor of his State, and his party was the
dominant party in the State, and, as far as such things
could be judged, he was in the line to become Governor
there, in one of the most dominant States of our Central
West. He said: 'I went home to fix that thing up as far as
I could, and to get ready for it. But I had hardly reached
home and exchanged greetings, when my wife, who was an
earnest Christian woman, said to me that a few of them
had made a little covenant of prayer that I might become
a Christian.' He did not want her to know the experience
that he had just been going through, and so he said as
carelessly as he could, 'When did this thing begin, this
praying of yours?' She named the date. Then he did some
very quick thinking, and he knew as he thought back,

that it was the day on the calendar when that strange impression came to him for the first time.

"He said to me: 'I was tremendously shaken. I wanted to be honest. I was perfectly honest in not believing in God, and I thought I was right. But if what she said was true, then merely as a lawyer sifting his evidence in a case, it would be good evidence that there was really something in their prayer. I was terrifically shaken, and wanted to be honest, and did not know what to do. That same night I went to a little Methodist chapel, and if somebody had known how to talk with me, I think I should have accepted Christ that night.'

"Then he said that the next night he went back again to that chapel where meetings were being held each night, and there he kneeled at the altar, and yielded his great strong will to the will of God. Then he said, 'I knew I was to preach,' and he is preaching still in a Western State. That is half of the story. I also talked with his wife—I wanted to put the two halves together, so as to get the bit of teaching in it all—and she told me this. She had been a Christian—what you call a nominal Christian—a strange confusion of terms. Then there came a time when she was led into a full surrender of her life to the Lord Jesus Christ. Then she said, 'At once there came a great intensifying of desire that my husband might be a Christian, and we made that little compact to pray for him each day until he became a Christian. That night I was kneeling at my bedside before going to rest, praying for my husband, praying very earnestly, and then a voice said to me, 'Are you willing for the results that will come if your husband is converted?' The little message was so very distinct that she said she was frightened; she had never had such an experience. But she went on praying still more earnestly, and again there came the quiet voice, 'Are you willing for the consequences?' And again there was a sense of being startled, frightened. But she still went on praying, and wondering what this meant, and a third time the quiet voice came more quietly than ever as she described it, 'Are you willing for the consequences?'

"Then she told me she said with great earnestness, 'O God, I am willing for anything Thou dost think good, if only my husband may know Thee, and become a true Christian man.' She said that instantly, when that prayer came from her lips, there came into her heart a wonderful sense of peace, a great peace that she could not explain, a 'peace that passeth understanding,' and from that moment—it was the very night of the covenant, the night when her husband had that first strange experience—the assurance never left her that he would accept Christ. But all those weeks she prayed with the firm assurance that the result was coming.

"Where were the consequences? They were of a kind that I think no one would think small. She was the wife of a man in a very prominent political position; she was the wife of a man who was in the line of becoming the first official of his State, and she officially the first lady socially of that State, with all the honor that the social standing would imply. Now she is the wife of a Methodist preacher, with her home changed every two or three years, she going from this place to that, a very different social position, and having a very different income than she would otherwise have had. Yet I never met a woman who had more of the wonderful peace of God in her heart, and of the light of God in her face than that woman."

And Mr. Gordon's comment on that incident is this:

"Now, you can see at once that there was no change in the purpose of God through that prayer. The prayer worked out His purpose; it did not change it. But the woman's surrender gave the opportunity of working out the will that God wanted to work out. If we might give ourselves to Him and learn His will, and use all our strength in learning His will and bending to His will, then we would begin to pray, and there is simply nothing that could resist the tremendous power of the prayer. Oh, for more men who will be simple enough to get in touch with God, and give Him the mastery of the whole life, and learn His will, and then give themselves, as Jesus gave Himself, to the sacred service of intercession!"

To the man or woman who is acquainted with God and who knows how to pray, there is nothing remarkable in the answers that come. They are sure of being heard, since they ask in accordance with what they know to be the mind and the will of God. Dr. William Burt, Bishop of Europe in the Methodist Episcopal Church, tells that a few years ago, when he visited their boys' school in Vienna, he found that although the year was not up, all available funds had been spent. He hesitated to make a special appeal to his friends in America. He counseled with the teachers. They took the matter to God in earnest and continued prayer, believing that He would grant their request. Then days later Bishop Burt was in Rome, and there came to him a letter from a friend in New York, which read substantially thus: "As I went to my office on Broadway one morning [and the date was the very one on which the teachers were praying], a voice seemed to tell me that you were in need of funds for the Boys' School in Vienna. I very gladly enclose a check for the work." The check was for the amount needed. There had been no human communication between Vienna and New York. But while they were yet speaking God answered them.

Some time ago there appeared in an English religious weekly the report of an incident narrated by a well-known preacher in the course of an address to children. He was able to vouch for the truth of the story. A child lay sick in a country cottage, and her younger sister heard the doctor say as he left the house, "Nothing but a miracle can save her." The little girl went to her money box, took out the few coins it contained, and in perfect simplicity of heart went to shop after shop in the village street, asking, "Please, I want to buy a miracle." From each she came away disappointed. Even the local pharmacist had to say, "My dear, we don't sell miracles here." But outside his door two men were talking and had overheard the child's request. One was a great doctor from a London hospital, and he asked her to explain what she wanted. When he understood the need, he hurried with her to the cottage, examined the sick girl, and said to the mother: "It is true—only a miracle can save her, and it must be performed at once." He got his instruments, performed the operation, and the patient's life was saved.

D. L. Moody gave this illustration of the power of prayer: "While in Edinburgh, a man was pointed out to me by a friend, who said: 'That man is chairman of the Edinburgh Infidel Club.' I went and sat beside him and said, 'My friend, I am glad to see you in our meeting. Are you concerned about your welfare?'

" 'I do not believe in any hereafter.'

" 'Well, just get down on your knees and let me pray for you.'

" 'No, I do not believe in prayer.'

"I knelt beside him as he sat, and prayed. He made a great deal of sport of it. A year after I met him again. I took him by the hand and said: 'Hasn't God answered my prayer yet?'

" 'There is no God. If you believe in one who answers prayer, try your hand on me.'

" 'Well, a great many are now praying for you, and God's time will come, and I believe you will be saved yet.'

"Some time afterwards I got a letter from a leading barrister in Edinburgh telling me that my infidel friend had come to Christ, and that seventeen of his club men had followed his example.

"I did not know *how* God would answer prayer, but I knew He would answer. Let us come boldly to God."

Robert Louis Stevenson tells a vivid story of a storm at sea. The passengers below were greatly alarmed as the waves dashed over the vessel. At last one of them, against orders, crept to the deck and came to the pilot, who was lashed to the wheel which he was turning without flinching. The pilot caught sight of the terror-stricken man, and gave him a reassuring smile. The passenger went below and comforted the others by saying, "I have seen the face of the pilot, and he smiled. All is well."

That is how we feel when through the gateway of prayer we find our way into the Father's presence. We see His face, and we know that all is well, since His hand is on the helm of events, and "even the wind and the sea obey him" (Mk 4:41). When we live in fellowship with Him, we come with confidence into His presence, asking in the full confidence of receiving and of meeting with the justification of our faith.

Let your hearts be much set on revivals of religion. Never forget that the churches have hitherto existed and prospered by revivals; and that if they are to exist and prosper in time to come, it must be by the same cause which has from the first been their glory and defence.

JOEL HAWES

If any minister can be satisfied without conversions, he shall have no conversions.

C. H. SPURGEON

I do not believe that my desires for a revival were ever half so strong as they ought to be; nor do I see how a minister can help being in a "constant fever" when his Master is dishonoured and souls are destroyed in so many ways.

EDWARD PAYSON

An aged saint once came to the pastor at night and said: "We are about to have a revival." He was asked why he knew so. His answer was, "I went into the stable to take care of my cattle two hours ago, and there the Lord has kept me in prayer until just now. And I feel that we are going to be revived." It was the commencement of a revival.

H. C. FISH

12

REVIVALS PART OF THE DIVINE PLAN

IT HAS BEEN SAID that the history of revivals is the history of religion, and no one can study their history without being impressed with their mighty influence upon the destiny of the race. To look back over the progress of the divine Kingdom upon earth is to review revival periods which have come like refreshing showers upon dry and thirsty ground, making the desert to blossom as the rose, and bringing new eras of spiritual life and activity just when the Church had fallen under the influence of the apathy of the times, and needed to be aroused to a new sense of her duty and responsibility. "From one point of view, and that not the least important," writes Principal Lindsay, in *The Church and the Ministry in the Early Centuries,* "the history of the Church flows on from one time of revival to another, and whether we take the awakenings in the old Catholic, the medieval, or the modern Church, these have always been the work of men specially gifted with the power of seeing and declaring the secrets of the deepest Christian life, and the effect of their work has always been proportionate to the spiritual receptivity of the generation they have spoken to."

As God, from the beginning, has wrought prominently through revivals, there can be no denial of the fact that revivals are a part of the divine plan. The Kingdom of

our Lord has been advanced in large measure by special
seasons of gracious and rapid accomplishment of the work
of conversion, and it may be inferred, therefore, that the
means through which God has worked in other times will
be employed in our time to produce similar results.

"The quiet conversion of one sinner after another, under the ordinary ministry of the Gospel," says one writer
on the subject, "must always be regarded with feelings of
satisfaction and gratitude by the ministers and disciples
of Christ; but a periodical manifestation of the simultane-
ous conversion of thousands is also to be desired, because
of its adaptation to afford a visible and impressive dem-
onstration that God has made that same Jesus, who was
rejected and crucified, both Lord and Christ; and that, in
virtue of His Divine Mediatorship, He has assumed the
royal sceptre of universal supremacy, and 'must reign till
all his enemies be made his footstool.' It is, therefore,
reasonable to expect that, from time to time, He will repeat that which on the day of Pentecost formed the con-
clusive and crowning evidence of His Messiahship and
Sovereignty; and, by so doing, startle the slumbering souls
of careless worldings, gain the attentive ear of the unconverted, and, in a remarkable way, break in upon those
brilliant dreams of earthly glory, grandeur, wealth, power
and happiness, which the rebellious and God-forgetting
multitude so fondly cherish. Such an outpouring of the
Holy Spirit forms at once a demonstrative proof of the
completeness and acceptance of His once offering of Himself as a sacrifice for sin, and a prophetic 'earnest' of the
certainty that He 'shall appear the second time without
sin unto salvation,' to judge the world in righteousness."

And that revivals are to be expected, proceeding, as
they do, from the right use of the appropriate means,

is a fact which needs not a little emphasis in these days, when the material is exalted at the expense of the spiritual, and when ethical standards are supposed to be supreme. That a revival is not a miracle was powerfully taught by Charles G. Finney. There might, he said, be a miracle among its antecedent causes, or there might not. The apostles employed miracles simply as a means by which they arrested attention to their message, and established its divine authority. "But the miracle was not the revival. The miracle was one thing; the revival that followed it was quite another thing. The revivals in the Apostles' days were connected with miracles, but they were not miracles." All revivals are dependent upon God, but in revivals, as in other things, He invites and requires the assistance of man, and the full result is obtained when there is cooperation between the divine and the human. In other words, to employ a familiar phrase, God alone can save the world, but God cannot save the world alone. God and man unite for the task, the response of the divine being invariably in proportion to the desire and the effort of the human.

This cooperation, then, being necessary, what is the duty which we, as co-workers with God, are required to undertake? First of all, and most important of all—the point which we desire particularly to emphasize—we must give ourselves to prayer. "Revivals," as Dr. J. Wilbur Chapman reminds us, "are born in prayer. When Wesley prayed, England was revived; when Knox prayed, Scotland was refreshed; when the Sunday school teachers of Tannybrook prayed, 11,000 young people were added to the Church in a year. Whole nights of prayer have always been succeeded by whole days of soul-winning."

When D. L. Moody's church in Chicago lay in ashes, he

went over to England in 1872, not to preach, but to listen to others preach while his new church was being built. One Sunday morning he was prevailed upon to preach in a London pulpit. But somehow the spiritual atmosphere was lacking. He confessed afterward that he never had such a hard time preaching in his life. Everything was perfectly dead, and, as he vainly tried to preach, he said to himself, "What a fool I was to consent to preach! I came here to listen, and here I am preaching." Then the awful thought came to him that he had to preach again at night, and only the fact that he had given the promise to do so kept him faithful to the engagement.

But when Mr. Moody entered the pulpit at night and faced the crowded congregation, he was conscious of a new atmosphere. "The powers of an unseen world seemed to have fallen upon the audience." As he drew toward the close of his sermon, he became emboldened to give out an invitation; and as he concluded, he said, "If there is a man or woman here who will tonight accept Jesus Christ, please stand up." At once about 500 people rose to their feet. Thinking that there must be some mistake, he asked the people to be seated, and then, in order that there might be no possible misunderstanding, he repeated the invitation, couching it in even more definite and difficult terms. Again the same number rose. Still thinking that something must be wrong, Mr. Moody, for the second time, asked the standing men and women to be seated, and then he invited all who really meant to accept Christ to pass into the vestry. Fully 500 people did as requested, and that was the beginning of a revival in that church and neighborhood. It brought Mr. Moody back from Dublin, a few days later, that he might assist the wonderful work of God.

The sequel, however, must be given, or our purpose in relating the incident will be defeated. When Mr. Moody preached at the morning service, there was a woman in the congregation who had an invalid sister. On her return home she told the invalid that the preacher had been a Mr. Moody from Chicago, and on hearing this the invalid sister turned pale. "What," she said, "Mr. Moody from Chicago! I read about him some time ago in an American paper, and I have been praying God to send him to London, and to our church. If I had known he was going to preach this morning I would have eaten no breakfast. I would have spent the whole time in prayer. Now, sister, go out of the room, lock the door, send me no dinner; no matter who comes, don't let them see me. I am going to spend the whole afternoon and evening in prayer." And so when Mr. Moody stood in the pulpit that had been like an ice chamber in the morning, the bedridden saint was holding him up before God, and God, who ever delights to answer prayer, poured out His Spirit in mighty power.

The God of revivals, who answered the prayer of His child for Mr. Moody, is willing to hear and to answer the faithful, believing prayers of His people today. Wherever God's conditions are met, there the revival is sure to fall. Professor Thomas Nicholson of Cornell College relates an experience on his first circuit that impresses anew the old lesson of the place of prayer in the work of God.

There had not been a revival on that circuit in years, and things were not spiritually hopeful. During more than four weeks the pastor had preached faithfully, visited from house to house, in stores, shops, and out-of-the-way places, and had done everything he could. The fifth Monday night saw many of the official members at lodges, but only a corporal's guard at the church.

From that meeting the pastor went home, cast down, but not in despair. He resolved to spend that night in prayer. "Locking the door, he took Bible and hymn book and began to inquire more diligently of the Lord, though the meetings had been the subject of hours of earnest prayer. Only God knows the anxiety and the faithful, prayerful study of that night. Near the dawn a great peace and a full assurance came that God would surely bless the plan which had been decided upon, and a text was chosen which he felt sure was of the Lord. Dropping upon the bed, the pastor slept about two hours, then rose, hastily breakfasted, and went nine miles to the far side of the circuit to visit some sick people. All day the assurance increased.

"Toward night a pouring rain set in, the roads were heavy and we reached home, wet, supperless, and a little late, only to find no fire in the church, the lights unlit, and no signs of service. The janitor had concluded that the rain would prevent the service. We changed the order, rang the bell, and prepared for war. Three young men formed the congregation, but in that 'full assurance' the pastor delivered the message which had been prayed out on the preceding night, as earnestly and as fully as if the house had been crowded, then made a personal appeal to each young man in turn. Two yielded, and testified before the meeting closed.

"The tired pastor went to a sweet rest, and next morning, rising a little later than usual, learned that one of the young men was going from store to store throughout the town telling of his wonderful deliverance, and exhorting the people to salvation. Night after night conversions occurred, until in two weeks we heard 144 people testify in forty-five minutes. All three points of that circuit saw a blaze of revival that winter, and family after family came into the church, until the membership was more than trebled.

"Out of that meeting one convert is a successful pastor in the Michigan Conference, another is the wife of one of the choicest of our pastors, and a third was in the ministry for a number of years, and then went to another denomination, where he is faithful unto this day. Probably none of the members ever knew of the pastor's night of prayer, but he verily believes that God somehow does for the man who thus prays, what He does not do for the man who thus prays, what He does not do for the man who does not pray, and he is certain that 'more things are wrought by prayer than this world dreams of.'"

All the true revivals have been born in prayer. When God's people become so concerned about the state of religion that they lie on their faces day and night in earnest supplication, the blessing will be sure to fall.

It is the same all down the ages. Every revival of which we have any record has been bathed in prayer. Take, for example, the wonderful revival in Shotts (Scotland) in 1630. The fact that several of the then persecuted ministers would take part in solemn convocation having become generally known, a vast concourse of godly persons assembled on this occasion from all quarters of the country, and several days were spent in social prayer, preparatory to the service. In the evening, instead of retiring to rest, the multitude divided themselves into little bands, and spent the whole night in supplication and praise. The Monday was consecrated to thanksgiving, a practice not then common, and proved the great days of the feast. After much entreaty, John Livingston, chaplain to the Countess of Wigtown, a young man and not ordained,

agreed to preach. He had spent the night in prayer and
conference; but as the hour of assembling approached, his
heart quailed at the thought of addressing so many aged
and experienced saints, and he actually fled from the duty
he had undertaken. But just as the kirk of Shotts was
vanishing from his view, those words, "Was I ever a barren
wilderness or a land of darkness?" were borne in upon his
mind with such force as compelled him to return to the
work. He took for his text Ezekiel 36:25-26 and discoursed
with great power for about two hours. Five hundred conversions were believed to have occurred under that one
sermon, thus prefaced by prayer. "It was the sowing of a
seed through Clydesdale, so that many of the most eminent Christians of that country could date their conversion, or some remarkable confirmation of their case, from
that day."

Of Richard Baxter it has been said that "he stained his
study walls with praying breath; and after becoming thus
anointed with the unction of the Holy Ghost he sent a
river of living water over Kidderminster." Whitefield
once thus prayed, "O Lord, give me souls or take my
soul." After much closet pleading, "he once went to the
Devil's fair and took more than a thousand souls out of
the paw of the lion in a single day."

Mr. Finney says: "I once knew a minister who had a
revival fourteen winters in succession. I did not know
how to account for it till I saw one of his members get up
in a prayer meeting and make a confession. 'Brethren,'
he said, 'I have been long in the habit of praying every
Saturday night till after midnight for the descent of the
Holy Ghost among us. And now, brethren (and he began
to weep), I confess that I have neglected it for two or

three weeks.' The secret was out. That minister had a praying church."

And so we might go on multiplying illustration upon illustration to show the place of prayer in revival and to demonstrate that every mighty movement of the Spirit of God has had its source in the prayer chamber. The lesson of it all is this: that as workers together with God we must regard ourselves as in not a little measure responsible for the conditions which prevail around us today. Are we concerned about the coldness of the Church? Do we grieve over the lack of conversions? Does our soul go out to God in midnight cries for the outpouring of His Spirit?

If not, part of the blame lies at our door. If we do our part, God will do His. Around us is a world lost in sin, above us is a God willing and able to save; it is ours to build the bridge that links heaven and earth, and prayer is the mighty instrument that does the work.

And so the old cry comes to us, with insistent voice, "Pray, brethren, pray."

Lord Jesus, cause me to know in my daily experience the glory and sweetness of Thy name, and then teach me how to use it in my prayer, so that I may be even like Israel, a prince prevailing with God. Thy name is my passport, and secures me access; Thy name is my plea, and secures me answer; Thy name is my honour and secures me glory. Blessed Name, Thou art honey in my mouth, music in my ear, heaven in my heart, and all in all to all my being!

C. H. SPURGEON

I do not mean that every prayer we offer is answered exactly as we desire it to be. Were this the case, it would mean that we would be dictating to God, and prayer would degenerate into a mere system of begging. Just as an earthly father knows what is best for his children's welfare, so does God take into consideration the particular needs of His human family, and meets them out of His wonderful storehouse. If our petitions are in accordance with His will, and if we seek His glory in the asking, the answers will come in ways that will astonish us and fill our hearts with songs of thanksgiving. God is a rich and bountiful Father, and He does not forget His children, nor withhold from them anything which it would be to their advantage to receive.

J. KENNEDY MACLEAN

13

CHRIST, OUR EXAMPLE IN PRAYER

THE EXAMPLE of our Lord in the matter of prayer is one which His followers might well copy. Christ prayed much and He taught much about prayer. His life and His works, as well as His teaching, are illustrations of the nature and necessity of prayer. He lived and labored to answer prayer. But the necessity of importunity in prayer was the emphasized point in His teaching about prayer. He taught not only that men must pray, but that they must persevere in prayer.

He taught in command and precept the idea of energy and earnestness in praying. He gives to our efforts gradation and climax. We are to ask, but to the asking we must add seeking, and seeking must pass into the full force of effort in knocking. The pleading soul must be aroused to effort by God's silence. Denial, instead of abating or abashing, must arouse its latent energies and kindle anew its highest ardor.

In the Sermon on the Mount, in which He lays down the cardinal duties of His religion, He not only gives prominence to prayer in general and secret prayer in particular, but He sets apart a distinct and different section to give weight to importunate prayer. To prevent any discouragement in praying, He lays as a basic principle the fact of God's great fatherly willingness—that God's willingness to answer our prayers exceeds our willingness to give good and necessary things to our children, just as far as God's ability, goodness, and perfection exceed our infirmities and evil. As a further assurance and stimulant to prayer, Christ gives the most positive and iterated assurance of answer to prayers. He declares: "Ask, and it shall be given you; seek, and ye shall find; knock, and it shall be opened unto you" (Mt 7:7). And to make assurance doubly sure, He adds: "For every one that asketh receiveth; and he that seeketh findeth; and to him that knocketh it shall be opened" (v. 8).

Why does He unfold to us the Father's loving readiness to answer the prayer of His children? Why does He asseverate so strongly that prayer will be answered? Why does He repeat that positive asseveration six times? Why does Christ on two distinct occasions go over the same strong promises, iterations, and reiterations in regard to the certainty of prayer being answered? Because He knew that there would be delay in many an answer which would call for importunate pressing and that if our faith did not have the strongest assurance of God's willingness to answer, delay would break it down. And that our spiritual sloth would come in, under the guise of submission, and say it is not God's will to give what we ask, and so we would cease praying and lose our case. After Christ has put God's willingness to answer prayer in a very clear and strong light, He then urges to importunity, and that every unanswered prayer, instead of abating our pressure, should only increase intensity and energy. If asking does not get, let asking pass into the settled attitude and spirit of seeking. If seeking does not secure the answer, let seeking pass on to the more energetic and clamorous plea of knocking. We must persevere till we get it. There will be no failure here if our faith does not break down.

As our great example in prayer, our Lord puts love as a primary condition—a love that has purified the heart from all the elements of hate, revenge, and ill will. Love is the supreme condition of prayer, a life inspired by love. Chapter 13 of 1 Corinthians is the law of prayer as well as the law of love. The law of love is the law of prayer, and to master this chapter from the epistle of Paul is to learn the first and fullest condition of prayer.

Christ taught us also to approach the Father in His name. That is our passport. It is in His name that we are to make our petitions known. "Verily, verily, I say unto you, He that believeth on me, the works that I shall do he shall do also; and greater works than these shall he do; because I go unto the Father. And whatsoever ye shall ask in my name, that will I do, that the Father may be glorified in the Son. If ye shall ask me anything in my name, that will I do" (Jn 14:12-14) .

How wide and comprehensive is that *whatsoever!* There is no limit to the power of that name. "Whatsoever ye shall ask." That is the divine declaration, and it opens up to every praying child a vista of infinite resource and possibility.

And that is our heritage. All that Christ has may become ours if we obey the conditions. The one secret is prayer. The place of revealing and of equipment, of grace and of power, is the prayer chamber, and as we meet there with God we shall not only win our triumphs but we shall also grow in the likeness of our Lord and become His living witnesses to men.

Without prayer the Christian life, robbed of its sweetness and its beauty, becomes cold and formal and dead; but rooted in the secret place where God meets and walks and talks with His own, it grows into such a testimony of divine power that all men will feel its influence and be touched by the warmth of its love. Thus, resembling our Lord and Master, we shall be used for the glory of God and the salvation of our fellowmen.

And that, surely, is the purpose of all real prayer and the end of all true service.

A man may pray night and day and deceive himself, but no man can be assured of his sincerity who does not pray. Prayer is faith passing into act. A union of the will and intellect realizing in an intellectual act. It is the whole man that prays. Less than this is wishing or lip work, a sham or a mummery.

If God should restore me again to health I have determined to study nothing but the Bible. Literature is inimical to spirituality if it be not kept under with a firm hand.

RICHARD CECIL

Our sanctification does not depend upon changing our works, but in doing that for God's sake which we commonly do for our own. The time of business does not with me differ from the time of prayer. Prayer is nothing else but a sense of the presence of God.

BROTHER LAWRENCE

Moody Press, a ministry of the Moody Bible Institute, is designed for education, evangelization and edification. If we may assist you in knowing more about Christ and the Christian life, please write us without obligation to: Moody Press, c/o MLM, Chicago, Illinois 60610.